Dr. Katz's

Me At a Glance

Created by Jonathan Katz and Tom Snyder

Written by Glenn Eichler

Illustrated by James Fagerquist

Original Character Design
by Annette LeBlanc Cate

COMEDY CENTRAL

POCKET BOOKS

HAIRLINE ONLINE

Digital Follicular Imaging and Fabrication for the Twenty-First Century

Dear Mr. Katz,

Thank you for your inquiry into HAIRLINE ONLINE. We are pleased to enclose your complimentary digital imaging sheet featuring six proposed styles of Hair Enhancement. These Enhancements, digitally superimposed upon a computer-generated version of the photograph supplied by you, were chosen by our digital psychographic selection system based upon your age, interests and belief system, as reflected in your completed questionnaire.

Please note that while a two-dimensional digital picture may reproduce an image, it cannot begin to reflect the immediate, dramatic improvements in perceived attractiveness and vigor projected by a HAIRLINE ONLINE Hair Enhancement. With a HAIRLINE ONLINE Hair Enhancement securely affixed to your head, you will see an instantaneous increase in your own personal magnetism and the respect of others — whether on the job, or "after hours" in the pursuit of leisure. I have been wearing a HAIRLINE ONLINE Hair Enhancement for more than five years now, and recently remarried for the third time — my first marriage since obtaining the Enhancement. My first wife was an accounts receivable clerk. My second wife had something or other to do with office furniture. My new wife is an aerobics instructor. See the difference!

Please look over the enclosed printout carefully. Think about how a vibrant new cranial profile would benefit you. Then call HAIRLINE ONLINE or visit our Web site *today* and let us begin the process of digitally changing your life!

Sincerely,

William L. Siberski
President
Hairline Online

Find out if Ben knows anything about how they got my picture.

HAIRLINE ONLINE

Digital Follicular Imaging and Fabrication for the Twenty-First Century

LANCE ORNSTEIN

Dear Jonathan,

   I can't tell you how tickled I was to run into you in the bookstore the other day. (I was tickled just to *recognize* you! How many years has it been since grad school — ten? Fifteen? Last time I saw you the old scalp-to-hair ratio was a lot different, that's for sure! But don't worry about that — you look fantastic, you really do. Very distinguished. I'm sure if my hair ever started to recede I wouldn't look half as good.) And to think I almost missed you when you ducked down behind that big stack of "Politically Correct Ethnic Slurs" books to tie your shoelace — and what if I hadn't kept calling your name over and over after you failed to respond the first time?! I hope the ear infection clears up soon (though I still think you should go see a sawbones and get that fluid drained).¡

   Actually it's pretty fluky that I happened to be in your neck of the woods at all. Well, not *that* fluky, considering all the campuses in this area, and how busy I've been on the lecture tour circuit. No matter how many times it happens to me, it never fails to amaze — you sit chained to a desk for months writing a book, and then a few weeks after it finally comes out and hits the best-seller list, you find yourself making ten times more money *talking* to people than you ever did *writing* for them. Of course the PBS series didn't hurt, but I chalk that bit of serendipity up to scheduling — on Tuesday nights there's simply no competition to speak of. I'm sure if "Baywatch" had been available anywhere on the dial, this wheezy old therapist couldn't have convinced ten *thousand* viewers to spend thirteen hours with him, never mind ten *million*. Next year they want to put me up against "Friends," but I told them that if they try that, I'll walk. I will, too. As far as I'm concerned, I've *done* television.

   Anyway, what I started to say was that it's a fluke that I was there because I wasn't lecturing at all — I'd just flown in for the afternoon to pick up some silly honorarium at one of the universities, and if my flight out hadn't been delayed, we never would have run into each other. I'm so sorry you had to run before we got a chance to catch up, because I'm dying to find out what you've been up to. Won't you write back and let me know? There's no friend like an old friend, and I'm sure that when we compare notes, we'll find a lot of commonality in our experiences since grad school.

   Now for the good news: I'm pretty sure I'll be back in your area this summer. I think I told you about the stage musical I've been working on with "Sir Andy" (Andrew Lloyd Webber — he *hates* being called that!) on the life of Sigmund Freud. Well, it looks as though we'll be workshopping it around your way before we start our pre-Broadway tour. I'll probably be crazy with rewrites and press interviews, but it would mean a tremendous amount to me if we could get together. I'd love for you to meet Crystal, too. Between us, I've had old wives and I've had young wives, and young wives are better! (I'm kidding, of course. Margaret was — *is* — a wonderful woman, and she did a great job with my "other" kids. We just grew apart.) So please do write or fax me back (E-mail's fine too). A pair of creaky headshrinkers like us need all the support we can get! (You can try calling, too, but I can't vouch for your chances there. With a schedule like mine, even my secretary has trouble getting me on the phone!)

   Looking forward to hearing *from* you and *about* you!

Cordially,

Lance

Lance Ornstein, M.D., Ph.D.
LO:rt
(Dictated but not read)

Must stop carrying this around! Not healthy!
Also, look into cheap places to spend summer abroad.

Opera World Magazine

"O beauty!"

Frank Atkinson
Intern to the Assistant Editor

Dr. Jonathan Katz
1124 North Sanchez Avenue

Dear Dr. Katz:

Thank you very much for your article proposal, "Are the Three Tenors Codependent?" It was read with much interest here. Unfortunately, *Opera World* is a magazine dedicated to celebrating the beauty and artistry of opera, not tearing at its foundation with rumor and innuendo. Our goal is to whisk our readers *away* from the tawdry cares of their day-to-day lives — to capture in print, if you will, that enchanted moment when the mastery of the musicians and the conductor, the set and costume designers, and of course the singers themselves combine to lift the audience and float them away in transcendence at the sheer beauty of which the human spirit is capable. I don't know if you've ever wept at the opera, Dr. Katz. My hunch, based on your article's premise ("Take away the orchestra and the tuxedos and you've got three chubby little boys, each one trying to show Mommy that *he* deserves the extra Mallomar") is that you haven't.

In any case, good luck and thank you for thinking of *Opera World*. I am sure you will find a more appropriate forum for your article. And by the way, the name of "Tenor Number Three," as you call him, is Jose Carreras, not Carrera. I believe the latter is some kind of automobile. I myself do not drive.

Sincerely,

Frank Atkinson

Frank Atkinson

Session Notes 1/11

Patient: Melissa R.

Melissa came in for her Monday session with usual complaint: weekend spent going to bars meeting new men (described first impressions as "cool," "really together," "great guy," etc.). Went to bed with three of them, by Sunday all three had "dumped" her (now descriptions change to "jerk," "selfish bastard," "pathetic little boy"). Asked her how she slept with three men in two nights — some kind of shift work, ha ha? She didn't laugh, said her weekends start with Thursday-night happy hour. Reflected to myself: when these guys see Melissa walk into a bar, they know they'll have a happy hour indeed. Decided not to share this observation. Instead felt obliged to caution her again about dangers of promiscuity. Her response: she makes each guy lather up with Liquid-Plumbr, wash off in her new shower (ten-jet high-powered disinfecting unit like in "Silkwood"), put on two condoms, and only then, if he isn't scalded too badly, goes to bed with him. She thinks these precautions may in some way contribute to the brevity of her relationships.

Melissa also depressed because Presidents' Day is coming up and extra day that weekend means she'll be sleeping with 25 percent more jerks than usual. She's tired of going out weekend after weekend and "finding every moron and bottom-feeder in a three-state radius." Gently suggested she try staying home one weekend. Got usual angry reaction: "What? And miss the chance to meet Mr. Right?" Then proposed a change of venue — instead of "meat market" bars, try meeting people at coffee lounge, poetry reading, perhaps bingo night at a local church. Unexpected reaction. I find it very unpleasant when my patients laugh at me. Particularly when the snorting starts.

Suggested Melissa's problem might be low self-esteem. She said she read "Smart Women Who Sleep with Smarmy Guys" too, she knows her problem is low self-esteem, and can't I do any better than that or should she save the money on our sessions and go talk to clerks at Barnes & Noble instead? Decided to change subject. Suggested we work up a profile of men she is attracted to and analyze common traits. "Let's start by eliminating those broad categories that don't interest you," I said. "What kind of man are you definitely not attracted to?" Apparently a trick question. She sat silent for many moments. Finally: "Well, I guess now that I think about it, there's no kind of man I'm not attracted to." Thoughtful pause. "Except you. Except you, Dr. Katz, you'd be the sort of man that doesn't appeal to me in any way whatsoever."

Will talk to Melissa about taking a break from therapy for a while.

FROM THE SKETCHPAD OF TONY LANG
Fine Art/Commercial Art/Rustproofing

Dear Dr. K.

Hope you don't mind, but during the session the other day i realized the difference between what you do and what a priest does: the priest doesn't charge you! And he doesn't drag your parents into it! Plus, he stops by when you're dying to say so long.

No, i'm kidding. it's all for a laugh, right, Doc? But it did get my doodling hand going, and i thought you might be amused by the result. See you Thursday!

Tony

Dr. Katz,
Professional Priest

Dr. Katz Professional Rabbi

Dr. Katz, Professional Mullah

Dr. Katz, Professional Fundamentalist

Dear Lance, It was great to see you, and even better to hear about all the fantastic things happening for you. It's always gratifying to learn that an old friend is doing so well. In a way, I feel your successes reflect well on all of us from the Class of 1969. Of course, some of us haven't managed to generate a cavalcade of self-aggrandizing "achievements" because we've been too busy treating people who need our help — you know, the thing we were trained to do? But I suppose we all make our own life choices.

~~Dear Lance, I hope you fly to Stockholm to accept the Nobel prize and during the banquet you choke on a pheasant bone.~~ Start over.

Dear Lance,
What a wonderful surprise running into each other the way we did. And as you pointed out, the odds were really stacked against it. I mean, there's your staggering schedule — congratulations on all those wonderful things that are happening for you, by the way — and then there's my busy schedule. Of course, we might easily have crossed paths at one of the colleges, since I've been guest lecturing at three of them this semester. (Boy, is my throat raw!) Otherwise, though, we almost certainly would have missed each other, since I'm so busy with my practice — I don't know whether it's word of mouth or what have you, but I find myself lately spending a good deal of time listening to the problems of internationally known diplomats and philosophers, and then of course there's my contract with the NBA to treat their first-round draft picks. Also, did I mention that I'm posing for one of the city's most prominent sculptors? Yes, he told me he rarely works in marble anymore, but for some reason when he saw me oh who am I kidding, draft picks and sculptors? Philosophers? Where'd I get _that_ one from? He'll see right through this in a second. I wish I'd written that self-help book. I'm a loser. No, no, no, I have nothing to be ashamed of. I can hold my head up high. He's the insecure one, that's why he has to do all that bragging. I'll just be cordial, tell him what I've been up to, wish him well. Upbeat all the way. I'm centered. I know who I am. Start over.

Dear Lance,
Go to hell, you arrogant bastard.
Leave this for later.

"Lonesome Train Blues"
By J. Katz, Professional Therapist

(Open tuning E)

Train, train, train
Here comes the train, train, train
Train gonna ride.
Yeah, train gonna ride.

Train, train, train
Here comes the train, train, train
Train gonna ride.
Yeah, train gonna ride.

If you don't see me outside the station,
It might be worth a look inside.
Yeah, a quick look inside.

I don't know — "bluesy" enough?

Dad, I think these people are onto something!

MAKE BIG MONEY AND NEVER BREAK A SWEAT!

Have you ever thought about taking your hard-earned life experience and turning it into BEAUTIFUL GREEN CASH? Well, you should! Consider these true-life stories:

• Every night after closing, Broadway dancer/waiter Trey Valienza would crawl under the tables in the restaurant where he worked, picking up napkins dropped by careless diners — until one night he said, "Enough is enough." He took an ordinary napkin, sewed some rubberized strips to the underside, and The Lapkin was born! Now the customers' napkins stay right where they're supposed to — and Trey *owns* the restaurant, thank you very much!

• Indiana housewife Mary Chatham admits that it was a walletful of maxed-out credit cards that forced her to create her own cosmetics using common caulking compound and her cats' fur balls — but now that we've helped her sell her makeup "recipes" to others, the Chatham credit rating is back to A-1!!

• It took corrections officer Bull Conroy decades to convince his superiors that a little psychology is better than a lot of beatings. We showed him how to adopt and market his "Shame and Blame" Negative Reinforcement System for use with schoolchildren, and now it's a favorite of educators throughout the land!!!

What common thread links these three very different success stories? Just this: these individuals took innovations *they had already developed for their own use* and, taking advantage of our marketing expertise, turned those innovations into sweet green cash with (no additional work) on their part! Don't *you* have a skill or special knowledge that *you* could convert into "found money"?

Reputable Video Marketing Inc. has been one of the region's leading producers of sales informational programming since mid-1995. We work with innovators and visionaries to create professional-looking sales informational programs (commonly if erroneously called "infomercials") ranging in length from five to sixty minutes. Working from our own state-of-the-art television studio/grain storage facility, Reputable Video Marketing Inc. works with *you* to:

• Conceptualize and write your program.
• Hire you the very best non-union crew and on-air talent available.
• Provide coaching, makeup and wardrobe should you decide to appear in the program yourself.
• Set up and staff your toll-free telephone ordering system.
• Store your excess grain or dry goods (in reasonable quantities) for up to 60 days.

Your specialized knowledge. *Our* multimedia expertise. Isn't it about time *you* were fairly compensated for your bright ideas? Reputable Video Marketing Inc. thinks so. Call 1-800-555-SILO and let us make your merchandising dreams come true!

Dad, we could do this using your specialized knowledge! Let's discuss!

I always hated flashbulbs.

Debating team finals. The year I developed a stammer.

Baby Ben exercises his legs.

Dad,
wasn't Mom in this
picture?

▼ TIME

Ben eating Banana
Split Cone at Land
of Wonder.
Two hours later he
threw it up all over
the backseat.

Dude
ranch,
Wyoming.
June 1976.
Local
hospital
well
equipped.

New Year's Eve at the therapists' Ball. Fun!

Mr. Jack Steele
Station Manager
WRRO "The Voice Of The People"

Dear Mr Steele:

I would like to register my deep unhappiness at my treatment last week by you and your staff. I am not naive enough to believe that you will apologize for what happened. My hope is that perhaps I may prevent it from happening to someone else.

I was pleased and a little flattered when your producer, Mr. Tommy Strong, called and asked me to appear as "an expert guest" on the Wes Powers Show. Because I am normally occupied in the early afternoon with my practice, I was not familiar with Mr. Powers's program, so I suppose I share a little of the blame for what happened. Nevertheless, I feel Mr. Strong misled me when he said Mr. Powers wanted to discuss "how therapy can help people in all walks of life." I should have realized something was wrong when he added, "You know, famous people, powerful people. Not just your average wacko," but I chalked it up to the normal callousness of youth.

In any case, I rescheduled my appointments for an entire afternoon, prepared notes, even dredged up some old voice-limbering exercises from my high school dramatics class. But the part I was about to play was no "Curly." It was no "Sir Lancelot." It was no "Professor Higgins." In short, it was The Fool. The very first question Mr. Powers asked me was not about how people in all walks of life can benefit from therapy. It was, "Who deserves intense shock treatment more — President Sex Hound, or his First Lady Macbeth? Let's open up the phones!" Unfortunately, that was the most rational moment of the program.

As you know, I am professionally trained to deal with disturbed individuals. But your listeners scare me. I was particularly concerned about the fellow who kept talking about his homemade guillotine, and the one who said that since the late 1980s he has been saving all his urine in jars. I don't know if you keep a record of who calls in to these programs, but perhaps you could steer some of the more tortured individuals into counseling programs. Or at least alert the police to their whereabouts.

In any case, Mr. Steele (by the way, does <u>anyone</u> at that station use the name he was born with?), I don't believe I am particularly thin-skinned. But I underwent a certain amount of inconvenience and personal sacrifice in order to appear on your program. To then be referred to repeatedly on the air for four hours as "Dr. Kook, Professional Nut Lover" was, in my opinion, inexcusable. The only bright spot in this nightmarish experience is that none of my patients seem to have been listening.

Sincerely,

Dr. Jonathan Katz
Professional Therapist

P.S. My son has asked me to add that he is a big fan of Dr. Virginia Garland, your Sunday night "intimacy adviser." I have no idea what an "intimacy adviser" is.

STOP HURTING YOUR OWN FEELINGS!

A Self-Help Book for Smart Men Who Say Stupid Things and Women Who, Wary of the Wolves, Choose to Run with the Wolverines

(Note to Self: Polish subtitle before submitting to publisher)

By Jonathan Katz, M.D.

1ST DRAFT

CHAPTER ONE: YOU ARE YOUR OWN BEST FRIEND, BUT SHOULD YOU LEND YOURSELF MONEY?

Today's men and women live and work under levels of stress that our cave-dwelling ancestors could only dream about, although chances are their dreams ran more toward topics like eating, staying warm and which end of the saber-tooth tiger had those nasty sharp things sticking out of it. Mind you, I'm speculating. But whatever their dreams were like, just as our ancestors found ways to cope with the stress of their time, e.g., through chest pounding, stalking mammoths, and attacking the tribe from across the stream and beating them to a bloody pulp, so must we find ways to cope with our stress in an era when such activities are often frowned upon by law enforcement officials and community leaders. I'm talking about teaching ourselves to COPE: Channel Our Psychological Exhaustedness into positive energy. (Actually, to be more precise, we need to COPPER: Channel Our Psychological and Physiological Exhaustedness Right. Or to be really exact about it, COPPERTONE: Channel Our Psychological and Physiological Exhaustedness, Revealing Tons Of New Energy.) This book will show you how to do just that.

The book you are now holding places special emphasis on the area of relationships. Why? Because our connectedness to other human beings is our most precious gift, the one that always fits and is never the wrong color. Picture a typical married couple of the 1990s. Often both spouses work, whether by choice or by economic necessity. Perhaps they must occasionally work late, or bring work home. They may have one or more school-age children who require their attention as well. It doesn't take a crystal ball to see that very quickly, the demands on their time -- to say nothing of their emotions and intellect -- can become so great as to border on overwhelming. Our couple may find that they have virtually no time to spend alone with each other; intimacy suffers. So that one afternoon, when they both arrive home on time to find, miraculously, that the children are out visiting friends or engaged in after-school activities, they may feel almost as if they must get acquainted with each other all over again. Perhaps they talk for a while over a glass of sauvignon blanc, relaxing on the living-room couch that they're usually too busy to enjoy. Maybe he tells a little joke and her bell-like laughter lingers in his ear. He hears something else in that laugh, the promise of secret delights to come, and he leans over and kisses her eyelids gently. Soon she is thrusting her tongue fervently, frantically, in and out of his mouth. She gasps as he tears open her blouse, revealing the snowy perfection of her perfectly shaped upturned breasts. Her pink nipples are sweet nectar in his mouth as he nibbles and bites, and then he is shuddering as she wraps her probing fingers around the swollen urgency of his manhood. "Now," she screams, "impale me!," and then a low moan escapes her glistening lips as he reveals the handcuffs he has been

Getting off track here. Come back to this later.

PORTRAITS OF A FAMILY

Perception Exploration Technique Yields Fascinating Results

THU FRI SAT

Clinical therapists at several teaching hospitals are reporting impressive results with a new perception-revelation technique in which family member are asked to draw simple sketches of themselves engaged in an activity, and then asked to draw similar sketches of each other.

"The disparity between how we perceive ourselves and how we are perceived is quite revealing," stated Dr. James Casey, who pioneered the technique. "It's not 'The Picture of Dorian Gray' so much as

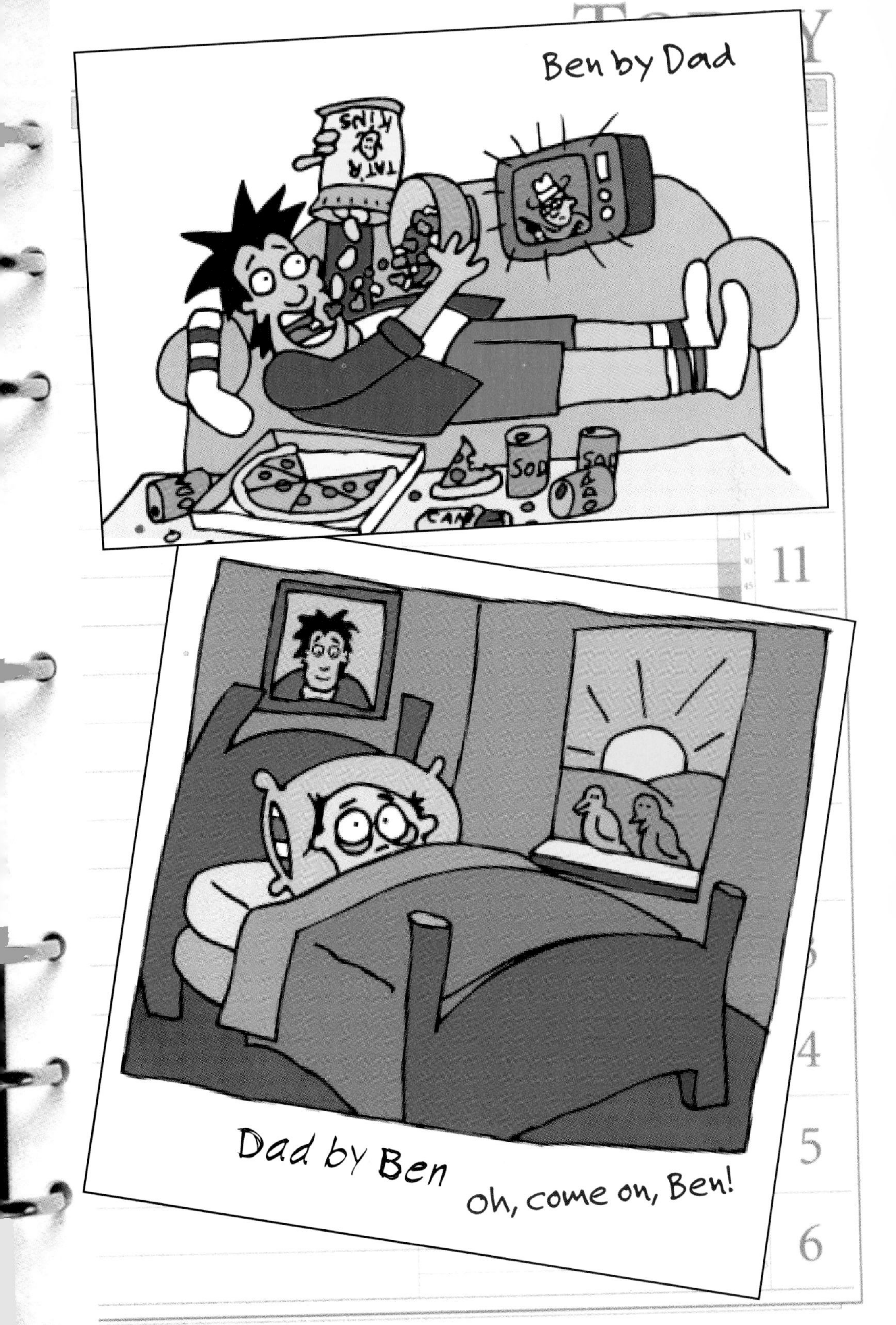
Ben by Dad
Dad by Ben
Oh, come on, Ben!

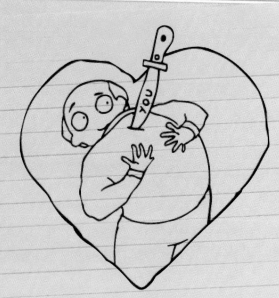

Dear Roz,

Happy birthday! I hope you don't mind a note instead of a card, but those things always seem so slick and impersonal — "Wishing you all the best on your special day," that sort of ersatz emotion — that I thought a note would just be more intimate. You don't mind me using the word "intimate," do you? Ha.

Anyway, how have you been? I hope things are going more or less the way you want. I say "more or less," of course, because expecting things to go exactly the way you want is simply not realistic. It's that constant cycle of setting unattainable goals and then, when you fail to achieve them, looking for someone to resent (almost like blowing out birthday candles and then getting angry when your wish doesn't come true) that probably caused you to begin viewing me as some sort of obstacle (what was the phrase you used? — oh yes, "dead weight") holding you back from your

6

Hi Roz, and happy birthday!

Just thought I'd drop you a note commemorating the day, and bring you up-to-date on how Ben and I have been doing. Well, actually, I guess you know how Ben's been doing, since you speak to him regularly, but you probably have no idea what I've been up to. I assume you're a little curious about how my life's been going, aren't you? I mean, it's hard to know for sure, since you always find some excuse for not getting on the phone to say hello to me, but I have to believe you care the tiniest bit. That is to say, when you spend years with someone, share your youth with them as it were, have a child with them, and then you won't even get on the phone to say hello, the sense of rejection for that person can really be quite crushing. Certainly not for me, I mean, with my training, but it could be for someone else, someone not schooled in the ways and means of human psychology. Myself, I just shrug that sort of thing off. Anyway, DO you want to know how I've been, or shouldn't I bore you, ha ha? I mean, don't you feel ANY inquisitiveness about the well-being of the man who fathered your son? I'm sorry, am I whining? I'm whining, aren't I? At least I'm not sniveling. That would be humiliating. I'm sniveling though, aren't I?

TIME ▼

Happy birthday, Roz!
Wishing you the all the best on your special day.

6

ALAKAZAM!
The Mystical Magazine of Magicians Everywhere

Dear Dr. Katz:

Thank you very much for sending us your article proposal, "Are Siegfried and Roy Codependent?" It was certainly one of the more offbeat proposals we have received in a long while and, in another time and place, would undoubtedly make for fascinating reading. Unfortunately, ALAKAZAM! cannot at this time give your article a home. For one thing, we are a small publication, a how-to, "tricks of the trade" magazine for aspiring magicians, dependent to a certain extent on the goodwill of the professional magic community. We simply cannot afford to alienate that community. If you've never gotten a magician angry, let me remind you that these are people who have no moral issue with the concept of taking a perfect stranger, imprisoning her in a dark, cramped box, and running half a dozen swords through it. You don't want to piss them off.

Secondly, ALAKAZAM! has neither the staff nor the space to handle the flood of inquiries we would receive if we acquired a reputation for publishing magicians' "dirty laundry." The David Copperfield queries alone would probably force us to move to bigger headquarters. Third — and I hope I am not speaking out of turn here — I minored in psychology at college, and it seems to me that your proposal relies on theses that are questionable at best, e.g., "It is an established psychological fact that entertainers who work with big cats are often trying to overcompensate for some physical 'smallness' of their own." On what do you base that statement, Doctor? I can't find anything like it in any of my old textbooks.

In any case, thank you very much for your interest in ALAKAZAM!, and please feel free to query us again. (Inside tip: right now we're working on a theme issue featuring sponge bunnies.)

Magically yours,

Jennifer Grady

Jennifer Grady
Associate Editor
and Classified Advertising Sales

FROM THE SKETCHPAD OF TONY LANG
Fine Art/Commercial Art/Rustproofing

Dear Dr. K.
Call me crazy — wait a minute, if you call me crazy, I think I'm in trouble! — but after our last session I got to musing, and it occurred to me that you really are a kind of warrior. Every day, armed with nothing but your intelligence and compassion, you wage a ferocious battle against your patients' personal demons. Then I thought, What am I talking about, the guy sits on his ass, listens

Dr. Katz, Professional Barbarian

Dr. Katz, Professional Jouster

to people bellyache, and gets a big fat check for it. He's figured out a way to get paid for doing what husbands do for free!

No, I'm pulling your leg. I'm a big admirer of yours, Doc, as if you didn't know. And I thought you might enjoy the results of all that heavy thinking I did: a few doodles that might bring a smile. Or maybe a career change, who knows! For you, I mean, not me!!

Ha ha! See you next time! Tony

Dr. Katz, Professional Mercenary

Dr. Katz, Professional Intergalactic Warrior

SUMMONS # 41611888392

NOTICE OF REQUIRED APPEARANCE
IN MUNICIPAL COURT

TRAFFIC SUMMONS

INFRACTION: ~~Illegal U-Tur~~
Three in

TOD

SAT

TIME ▼

7

JONATHAN KATZ, M.D.
1124 North Sanchez Avenue

Office of the Municipal Court
Traffic Division

Re: Summons # 41611888392

To whom it may concern:
I am writing in regard to the above-referenced summons,
in the hope that I may have the case dismissed without
submitting all involved to a time-wasting court appearance.
It appears that I am the victim of a case of mistaken
identity. I believe some youth, perhaps hopped up on drugs,
stole my car, took it for a joyride downtown, and returned it
to my home without my ever finding out about it.
I admit that this sounds far-fetched, and that you are
probably used to hearing far-fetched stories by people
trying to avoid paying tickets. But consider this: I have
been driving for more than thirty years without a single
moving violation. I am a responsible member of the community
with a long-standing therapy practice. Why, at 11 a.m. on a
Wednesday morning, would I be driving around on the opposite
side of town from my office, suddenly decide to start making
illegal U-turns — three in a row — and then, after being
pulled over by an officer, tell him I was trying to get the
attention of a young woman pedestrian?
In any case, I was with a patient at that time, who has
signed a statement to that effect on the back of this letter.
I accept responsibility for not securing my car as well as I
might have, and for leaving my license in the glove
compartment. If there's such a thing as a fine for negligent
auto security, I'll gladly pay that. But I would also like to
know if the traffic officer looked very carefully at the
photo on my license and compared it to the driver of the car.
As you can see by the enclosed photocopy, I have a very
distinctive hairline. Even if, by some crazy, one-in-a-
million coincidence, there was a facial resemblance, I'd bet
anything the driver's hair was different. I'd bet he
couldn't possibly have the listed date of birth, either.

I am anxious to clear this matter up so that I can go back to my patients and you can concentrate your efforts on finding the young hoodlum who is really responsible for this irresponsible driving. I wouldn't be surprised if it were someone from out of state.

Thank you very much for your time and trouble.

Sincerely,

Dr. Jonathan Katz

Dr. Jonathan Katz

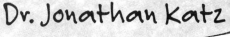

DRIVERS LICENSE

-04-6120

Dr. Jonathan Kat

Bruce Ratner
Ratner Auto World
Route 17

Dear Bruce,
I've got a quick question for you on my car's ignition lockout device. I understand that it disables the car if someone tries to start it without the original keys. Is there some way it can be set to disable the car against someone who has borrowed the original keys without asking? You know, like a family member? Thanks a lot.

Jonathan Katz

Jonathan,
You're not making sense, buddy
Bruce

"CHERRIES IN THE SNOW"
By J. Katz, Professional Therapist

(Moderate tempo ballad. Fingerpick.)

They walked the winter lane together
Cherries in the snow
Her tiny hand in his, he whispered
"Soon, soon, my love,
"Soon I must go"

She looked into his umber eyes
The tears began to flow
"Yes, yes I know," she whispered"
Soon, soon, my love,
Soon you must go"

The snow had o'ertaken the path
As sadness did their talk
He whispered sadly in her ear,
"You know, my love,"
It's getting hard to walk"

"I thought you had to leave," she said
"I pray you, make it swift,"
He said, "You're just not getting this,
Help, help, my love,
I think I'm stuck in a drift"

And soon two frigid lovers stood
Prepared — for love — to die,
"They'll find us in our last embrace,"
"Yes, yes, my love,"
Then the man with the plow came by.

Powerful. Could be a real showstopper. Let it build!

STOP HURTING YOUR OWN FEELINGS!

An Odyssey of Self-Realization for Personal Pilgrims
Who Want to Rediscover the Untrodden Land Within
Before the Tourists of Self-Doubt Get There

(Note to Self: Subtitle may need work)

By Jonathan Katz, M.D.

CHAPTER ONE: WHY ARE WE GIVEN AN INNER CHILD BUT NOT CHEAP, RELIABLE INNER CHILD CARE?

As a practicing therapist, I am privileged to work every day with fellow human beings trying to rid themselves of the obstacles standing between them and realizing their full potential. I use the word "privileged" advisedly -- because to me, having other men and women place that much trust in me is a privilege indeed. I often feel like an auto mechanic who repairs nothing but Rolls-Royces and Ferraris: each car brought into my shop is an expression of faith in my abilities, yet should I drop a wrench in the wrong place while working on one, the damage caused to the pistons could be irreparable. I do not always share this analogy with my patients.

It's no secret that today's frantic lifestyles can lead to copious amounts of stress. In a typical two-career family, mornings are a time of rushed preparation, not a gradual easing in to the day; add children to the mix and the morning routine begins to feel like a deliberately contrived test of endurance. It's as if some outside force is watching us shower, dress, bolt down breakfast, wake, feed, dress the children, and then get them off to school before doubling back to catch the train to work ourselves. Not a disinterested force, either. It almost feels like a malevolent force, a force whose eyes, sunk deep into their blackened sockets, have witnessed centuries of fear and horror. It's a force that roamed freely through the steaming swamp that occupied this ground when the earth was young. It's a force that claimed the lives of Native American infants sleeping in their tepees hundreds of years before the first white face appeared on the horizon. It's a force that sent smallpox raging through the starving settlers from England, claiming first the old and the frail, then the young and the strong, sparing no family, decimating their ranks, until the bodies piled up in the churchyard like cordwood because there weren't enough strong men left to bury them. It's a force that remained, hidden under the surface, watching through those same reptilian eyes, as the surveyors came, and then the men with their chain saws and their earthmovers and their cement mixers, and built the sleepy little suburb of Lawnwood.

Now Lawnwood is filled with the laughter of innocent children, the lazy gossip of old friends sitting around the pool, the sighs of lovers at sunset… and still it waits. But soon it will wait no more. Soon, as it has done again and again since there was no sound heard here but the cry of the mockingbird, it will rise to claim back this patch of ground. Necks will be broken, arms and legs severed inexplicably. Blameless young mothers will be mangled beyond recognition in seemingly impossible automobile accidents. Boys and girls will disappear, never to be heard from again.

It is coming.

It is coming for us.

And nothing we do can stop it.

I don't think this is going to reassure people. And I'm really scared. Put aside for now.

Cool Kidz

The Young People's Magazine

Dr. Jonathan Katz
1124 North Sanchez Avenue

Dear Dr. Katz:

Thank you for sending your article idea to *Cool Kids, the Young People's Magazine.* There is no doubt that your proposal, "Are the Intergalactic Super Defenders Codependent?," is one of the most unique ideas we have ever received. Unfortunately we will not be able to print your article. As you may know, the characters of the Intergalactic Super Defenders are copyrighted by Zambro Toys, all rights reserved, and any unauthorized work of fiction utilizing those characters is subject to lawsuit. At least I <u>hope</u> your article is meant as a work of fiction. Am I right also in guessing that your title of "Doctor" is one that you bestowed upon yourself? I have to believe no real therapist would make such statements as this: "Tiffany, the Pink Defender, clearly chafes at her 'traditional' female role. We see this in her unexpressed anger toward Melanie, the Orange Defender, and her subtle sexual advances toward Brad, the Golden Defender, whose gender ambiguity she senses on a visceral rather than intellectual level." I'm compelled to ask, "Dr." Katz: Have you ever actually watched the Super Defenders? Each afternoon they play video games for a while, then change into their uniforms, fight some costumed stunt performers, and then go back to playing video games. Surely all this "passive-aggressive enabling" and "libidinous role-playing" you mention are figments of your own imagination. Surely you don't actually believe there's something "neurotic, almost psychotic" about throwing a few fake punches at a bodybuilder in a lizard suit. And surely you don't mean to burden our readership of 8-to-14-year-olds — sophisticated though today's kids may be — with your own fevered fantasies concerning the Defenders (and, apparently, Brad in particular).

"Dr." Katz, *Cool Kids* is a magazine for children. In our pages the emphasis is on fun, but in our offices we take our responsibility very seriously. Your extraordinarily inappropriate article, were it to be published, could be very upsetting to our readers. It could actually drive some of them into therapy — or is that your ulterior motive after all, simply to drum up business for yourself? Have I gravely underestimated you?

If so, you are an insidious exploiter, an evil, evil man, and I implore you, sir: Leave the children alone!

Sincerely,

Victoria Martinez

Victoria Martinez
Features Editor

Hello! As part of my ongoing effort to provide you with the best therapy possible, I have devised the following Patient's Evaluation Form. Won't you take a few moments to fill it out at your convenience and drop it in the box in our reception area? This is an anonymous evaluation, so please <u>do not</u> write your name on the form. In addition, please don't ask Laura, my receptionist, to take the form from you. She has recently informed me of a skin condition that prevents her from handling paper.

1. How do you feel your therapy is progressing?

Really well. I'm able to undress in front of other men for the first time in my life. In fact, I've begun to enjoy it!

2. Do you feel that we are covering areas of importance?

Yes, but I'd like to get into more detail about <u>why</u> my father is such a bastard.

3. After a typical session, do you feel hope, despair, or other emotion(s)?

I don't feel emotions per se. But I do find that I have firm control over my bladder for up to two hours after a session. Two hours! Thanks Doc

4. What is the best thing about your therapy?

I have become master of my own destiny, and that feels great!

5. What is the worst thing about your therapy?

I worry constantly that something will happen to you and I'll have to lock myself back in my room.

6. If you could change one thing about our sessions, what would it be?

I'd like your permission to tape-record them and send them anonymously to my father. The football-watching troglodyte.

7. Are there any areas in which you think I, as your therapist, could improve?

Don't take this the wrong way, but that damned humming is infuriating.

8. If I told you that I had written a self-help book, do you think you'd be tempted to purchase it?

Maybe after it came out in paperback. Unless I could take it out of the library.

9. Do you enjoy fresh, hot coffee?

What?

10. Please use the space below for any additional comments you'd like to make.

I'd like to know that I'm putting a clause in my will naming you as guardian of my children. If I have an accident or anything, I won't have those poor defenseless babies falling into the hands of that monster who "raised" me! Assuming that one day I get married and <u>have</u> children, of course.

Troy Buchanan

6

Session Notes 3/14

Patient: Patient 'K'

Patient K arrived with usual cloak-and-dagger stuff: his driver parked two blocks away, he approached the building through alley, came up freight elevator, and used "secret buzzer code" on the doorbell — Laura supposed to clear waiting room of suspicious characters, reporters or voters when she hears buzz. Fortunately waiting room was empty, because as usual Laura didn't hear a thing.

Patient K very proud of these precautions. How much of this is prudence, how much paranoia? Yes, a U.S. senator, or any public figure, probably wise to be discreet about therapy. But if trying to be inconspicuous, why drive through downtown in a black stretch limo with American flags on each fender, honking at women on the street? No matter how far away you park? I commented positively to Patient K that at least he wasn't wearing one of those silly disguises. Response: "Look again, Dr. Katz. Look closely." I did. Saw nothing. He pointed at eyes: "Tinted contacts. My cleverest disguise yet. My normal eye color is green, but with these in, people think they're hazel." Decided that yes, this was paranoia, coupled with streak of good old-fashioned stupidity.

Asked how campaign progressing. He complained about staff's "lack of vision." Said he had come up with innovative ideas to generate crowd response. But when he floated concept of having bikini-clad lesbians at campaign stops, several advisers resigned on the spot. Ones who stayed also shot down his idea of campus

"Happy Hour" appearances featuring free draft beer ("Of course we're talking 100 percent American brewski") during speech. Strategists thought this unwise in light of Patient K's past legal problems. I nodded, said silent prayer for safety of these advisers.

Patient K cut session short, odd in light of pains he took to get here, but he explained: extremely critical budget vote in Senate today, affecting course of the nation for generations to come. He wanted to get home to watch C-SPAN and see how it turned out. As he gave special knock on the door to waiting room, signaling Laura to clear it — she heard nothing — my thoughts turned to Ben. Maybe he's right. Maybe Tahiti makes a lot of sense.

Dad,
What do you think of this script I've
written for your infomercial?
Feel free to be completely candid
with any positive comments that come
to mind.

Tired of long, drawn-out, expensive therapies?
Can you think of better ways to spend your time and money than
spending hour after hour, week after week talk-talk-talking
about your problems? Leery of so-called "wonder drugs" that
promise you peace of mind but <u>could</u> turn you into a crazed
postal worker?
Now <u>you</u> can get fantastic therapy results in just fifteen
minutes a day — <u>without</u> dangerous drugs or all that boring
talk! Just pop DR. KATZ'S FIFTEEN MINUTES A DAY TO MENTAL
HEALTH into your VCR, and you're on your way!

Hi. I'm Dr. Jonathan Katz, a well-respected therapist with a
thriving practice providing sensitive, affirming treatment to
otherwise ordinary people who just happen to be a few bricks
shy of a load. For a long time now I've dreamed of being able
to reach out and help people <u>beyond</u> my own fanatically loyal
group of patients. I'm talking about <u>using today's technology</u>
to bring therapy to people who didn't even know they needed
help — people like <u>you.</u>

"Me?" you may be saying. "I don't need therapy. Heck, I'm the
reason my entire family's in therapy." (Chuckle.) Well, maybe
you <u>are</u> one of the lucky ones who couldn't benefit from some
good psychological direction. But on the other hand — maybe
you <u>could</u>. Why not try this simple test you can take right now?
Grab a pencil or pen and jot down your answers to this
multiple-choice question. It's fun!

When I'm on the highway and another driver cuts me off, I
A feel a momentary twinge of annoyance, but then forget about
   it.
B curse, honk my horn and make an obscene gesture.
C go into a pattern of accelerating and decelerating so that I
   can slam into his rear bumper repeatedly.
D hate my mother.

The correct answer? Well, a <u>traditional</u> therapist would tell
you there are no "right" and "wrong" answers — that's how he
keeps you coming back week after week! But if you owned a copy
of DR. KATZ'S FIFTEEN MINUTES A DAY TO MENTAL HEALTH, you'd
already know that answers B,C and D indicate some unresolved

anger that <u>you</u> have to work on. <u>You</u> need DR. KATZ'S FIFTEEN MINUTES A DAY TO MENTAL HEALTH.

And answer A? "Feel a momentary twinge of annoyance, but then forget about it?" At first blush, you might think that's a reasonable, mature way to handle the situation. That's why I'm a therapist and you're not! The <u>truth</u> is that answer A indicates an elaborate mechanism of denial and emotional repression so powerful it will almost certainly result in an aneurysm down the road — unless you get yourself a copy of DR. KATZ'S FIFTEEN MINUTES A DAY TO MENTAL HEALTH, pronto! Think about it — do you want to see me, or the neurosurgeon? (Chuckle)

How does DR. KATZ'S FIFTEEN MINUTES A DAY TO MENTAL HEALTH work? It's easy. When you pop the tape into the VCR you'll see me — Jonathan Katz — seated in my actual chair in my actual office. I'll invite you to tell me how you've been feeling, and then, while you talk, I'll listen carefully — interrupting now and then with an "Mm-hm" or an "I see" or perhaps a gentle "How did that make you feel?" After fifteen minutes I'll tell you that our time is up and we'll both go our merry ways — me back to my little cardboard box, you out there to take on the world! See you next time!

How is DR. KATZ'S FIFTEEN MINUTES A DAY TO MENTAL HEALTH superior to traditional therapies?
· <u>I'm ready when you are.</u> The sessions are scheduled for your convenience, and I won't bill you if you cancel without notice.
· <u>We're on your turf.</u> No office full of intimidating Danish furniture and abstract prints to intimidate you (unless you have them in your own house).
· <u>I don't require your full attention.</u> Do you need to catch up on your ironing, the dishes, the treadmill? Do you like to have a little drink while you spill your guts? Go ahead. I'll never know.
· <u>You don't have to talk at all if you don't want to.</u> Is our conversation veering into painful territory? Or are you just not in the mood for it today? Clam up if you like. I won't even notice.
· <u>The session never drags on past the point where you run out of things to say.</u> There's only fifteen minutes of tape in the cassette. You have my word on it. See how easy it can be to get yourself emotionally toned and trim the '90s way? Get yourself DR. KATZ'S FIFTEEN MINUTES A DAY TO MENTAL HEALTH — you'd be crazy not to!
(Then we put the ordering info here.)

Ben, what infomercial?

BAUD COMPANY

Jacking in the World!

Dear New Subscriber:

Hello and welcome to BAUD COMPANY, America's premiere on-line service for computer users who don't want to know what they're doing. With your computer, the enclosed BAUD COMPANY installation disk and a major credit card (your own), you're ready to join the millions of computer users worldwide who have found excitement and satisfaction navigating the Internet for business, pleasure and celebrity autopsy photos. First, however, comes the fun part — choosing your online nickname! This is the name your cyberfriends will know you by, so it should reflect something about you — whether your occupation, personality, favorite hobby, identifying scars — the sky's the limit, so let yourself go! (Use of obscenity will result in immediate arrest and confiscation of computer equipment.)

Once you have chosen your on-line name, it's time to install BAUD COMPANY. First, locate the installation disk in this

Psych-Man
PsychoGuy
GoodLisner
Analize (sound obscene?)
N.L.lst
OurTimesUp
Bens Dad
BennysPa
LuvMySon
MoveOutBen
BenWontWork
FailedMySon
Luv2Listen
Thera-P
JungAtHeart
CapnStud
HooDooMan
BradPitt
Supportive
CareNShare
RufNReddy
SuperPecs
Washboard Abs
GroinPull

Want2Talk?
CybrShrink
ShrinkRap
Balladeer
Tunesmith
GuitarGod
LuvMyself
LikeMyself
SelfHatr
ThikDarkHair
Adonis
OpnUp2Me
TriathlonMan
BiathlonMan
AthlonMan
KingOShrinks
LoneWolf
KrazyKatz
LuckyInLuv
UnluckyInLuv
BustdMarriage
SelfSufficient
SingleAndOK
ReallyLonely

Ways I Can Improve As a Therapist

No Finger Drumming Ever!

Festive ties to mark major holidays

Replace waiting room issues of <u>Collier's</u> with something more contemporary

Increase sympathetic headshakes and grunts

Keychains: "I ♥ my patients"

Resist being judgmental — that's the police's job

Moist towelettes

No transistor radio no matter <u>how</u> close the pennant race

Check bathroom for graffiti <u>every</u> day

Piñata party for patients at Xmas?

More aggressive use of air freshener after Mrs. Henning's sessions

Use of air freshener <u>during</u> Mrs. Henning's sessions?

Watch the humming!

TO: LAURA

FROM: DR. K

RE: Five Ways We Can Improve the Office Ambience Together

1. A More Encouraging Phone Manner
   I spend a good deal of time trying to put patients at ease.
It almost feels like we're at "cross purposes" when they call
and you act like they're imposing. Last week Melanie Warnski
asked me if she had gotten you out of the shower. I think we
both know how the word "receptionist" makes you feel, and I try
very hard to respect that, but nonetheless I find it disturbing
that several of the patients have inquired as to whether I have
a private number they can dial and (I'm quoting now) "avoid the
security people" on the main number. As you know, Mr. Stevens
now refuses to call at all until I get my phone equipped with a
scrambler. Laura, I'm sure we can do better.

2. Acknowledging Ben's Presence
   I admit that Ben can be annoying when he has too much time
on his hands. I also grant that having too much time on his
hands is more or less a permanent condition for him. But when
Ben stands in front of your desk waving his arms, and you read
a paperback book as if there's nobody there, it frightens the
patients. More than one of them have dragged me out of the
inner office to ask me whether Ben was really there, or had
they only imagined him?

3. Greater Willingness to Call Out for Lunch
   Laura, you'll recall that I took very seriously your
complaint about having to dial 9 to get an outside line, and,
at significant expense to myself, had our phone system
replaced so you would no longer suffer that imposition. You'll
also, I hope, acknowledge that all the places we order lunch
from, being in the neighborhood, share our area code — so no
lunch call ever requires the dialing of more than seven digits.
On most days that call is the only time you are asked to use
your fingers on the job, so it's hard for me to believe it
aggravates your RSS as much as you say it does (see below). In
any case, when the patients hear me on the intercom pleading
with you to order lunch, it undermines my authority with them.
A couple of them have actually started bringing bag lunches for
me, which has proven highly embarrassing and extremely

unappetizing. Point to consider: if my authority is undercut, so is my effectiveness in treating patients, so their therapy is dragged out — which means you have to see them that many more times. And I know that's the last thing you want. Actually, that brings me to my next point:

4. The Patients Are Not Contagious and Shouldn't Be Treated As If They Were

Laura, I have pretty good instincts about people, and my instincts tell me that deep down you are a warm, caring person. I realize that one of the therapist's (and the therapist's assistant's) cardinal rules is never to get emotionally involved with the patients, and you have lived up to that rule 110 percent. But I'm concerned that you may have taken it a little too much to heart. I may get drummed out of the therapists' association for this, but I think it would be okay for you to smile at the patients when they come in, perhaps ask them how they are, how the weather is outside, etc. Even just simple eye contact would probably be much appreciated. And please, please don't use funny nicknames when announcing them. "Mr. Dumpty is here for his appointment" — no, no, no!

5. Get a Second Opinion on Your Repetitive Stress Syndrome

Please don't take this as a criticism of your doctor, but I'm still having trouble understanding how you developed Repetitive Stress Syndrome at all. Even <u>before</u> we eliminated the typing, note-taking and filing from your workload, I never asked you to spend more than ten minutes on any of those activities in a given day. Don't misinterpret me. I know you're doing a very important job just by being there to answer the patients' questions, direct them to the bathroom, tilt your head toward the closet, etc., and I certainly appreciate it. It's just that now, more than a year after we abolished virtually all finger movement from your job, and after you've been taking five hours off every week to go to physical therapy, I was hoping maybe you could ease back into some of the less strenuous finger-related activities, such as perhaps opening the mail.

Dr. K, All I see here are ~~five ways~~ I can improve the ~~office~~ ambience. Where are the ways ~~you~~ can improve the ~~office~~ ambience? Can't write any more now. My ~~fingers~~ are throbbing.

JONATHAN'S CAFÉ CAFFE

"Good coffee, good company, good feelings"

Hello greater Portland, and a sincere welcome to Jonathan's Café Caffe from your humble host, Jonathan Katz! Having spent 10 years in the urban jungle as a Professional Therapist, dreaming of the day I could move to Maine, kick back and open my own Coffee Bar, I'm delighted that that day has finally arrived! My wife _____ and I are proud to offer a handpicked selection of hot and cold beverages, an honest appreciation of your company, and hey — I may not be a Professional Therapist anymore, but if you've got a problem, your Coffee Bartender is here to listen!

The following beverages are available in traditional, decaffeinated, half-caffeinated, espresso grind, half-portion, double-portion and iced servings, from grounds dripped, pressed or perked, with cream, half-and-half, whole, 2%, 1% and nonfat milk, and/or with twirled rind segments from the following fruits: lemon, lime, grapefruit, kiwi, watermelon.*

JONATHAN'S JUST PLAIN CUPPA: You want coffee, we got coffee! None of that fruity pretentious Europo stuff for you — just a good solid 10-ounce cup of Joe. Do yourself a favor and skip the rest of the menu; it'll just aggravate you.

CAFFE LATTE: You like your desserts and you like 'em big. Here's the liquid version: dreamy, steamy coffee with plenty of that "fluffy" kind of milk. Like that hot chocolate your Mom used to make, with the caffeine kick you need to face life now that mom's gone.

CAFFE GRAN LATTE: For the coffee lover nonpareil!** Our biggest, most sumptuous Latte, for those who just can't get enough coffee. You really ought to consider whether all that coffee's good for you, though. Or is it really just a substitute for something else?

CAPPUCCINO: You really want a latte, but you're twenty pounds overweight and your spouse is watching. Order a smaller cappuccino instead, and congratulate yourself — you've shown moderation! Then order another when your better half goes to the bathroom. See, we can work it out!

MOCHA JAVA: A delicious Kenya-Kona-Jakarta-Jamaica blend laced with the rich, savory flavor of mocha! What's mocha? I haven't a clue!

MOCHACCINO: Cross a horse and a donkey, you get a mule. Cross mocha java with cappuccino, you get a mochaccino. Like a mule, it's incapable of reproducing. Unlike a mule, it's delicious!

ESPRESSO: Nobody better get in your way today. Nobody better screw around with you. Nobody better look at you the wrong way. 'Cause you're drinking Jonathan's Espresso, and you're fighting mad!***

FLAVORED COFFEES: For a change of pace, dip into our huge selection of flavored coffees! Vanilla, Hazelnut, Amaretto, Chocolate Graham Cracker, Fluffernutter, Tuna, Scotch-and-Water — they make me nauseous, but you're the customer!

And don't forget...

BENNY'S BETTER BUTTER COOKIES: Named for my son, who won't settle for second best. Pricey? Maybe. But if you care about supporting America's dairy farmers, this way's a lot tastier than a donation to Farm Aid!

JONATHAN'S BIG-BITE BISCOTTI: It's not stale — it's supposed to be like that!

Thanks for patronizing Jonathan's Cafe Caffe, come again soon — and enjoy the rest of your vacation/honeymoon/retirement/productive years!

*In season.   **Nonpareils extra.   ***We are prohibited by law from serving Jonathan's Espresso to employees of the United States Postal Service.

Dad, a coffee bar just seems so... I don't know. Why not go for something a little livelier? And when do I get to meet your wife, _____?

Hey Dad!
We could have a little brochure in your videotape like that one in the Star Wars tape where you can order the Han Solo chafing dish. Only they'd be products that enhance your Dr. Katz's Fifteen Minutes A Day To Mental Health experience! What do you think of these ideas?

Dr. Katz's Dream Jotter System — Dream interpretation is vital to therapy — but you can't analyze what you can't remember! That's why we've created Dr. Katz's Dream Jotter System — a pad, a pencil and a flashlight. The pencil's a reliable No. 2 just like the one you used in grade school, but with the Dr. Katz logo. The pad's got lines for keeping that wobbly post-sleep handwriting on course. And you'll thank me for the flashlight, I guarantee! Because I don't care how "smart" or "important" or "together" you are — when you wake up in the middle of the night, it's dark out! That's a fact of life!!!

Dr. Katz's Be Your Own Best Friend Hand Mirror — Whether for combing your hair, fixing your makeup, or checking for growths in hard-to-reach places, everyone needs a hand mirror! And since therapy is all about liking what you see in that mirror, why not turn "mirror time" into "self-affirming time?" Our mirror has these positive words embossed on its frame: "Hey! Look there! It's my best friend! Hello, best friend!" And that simple message says it all.

Dr. Katz's Humorous Tee Shirts — Not technically an aid to therapy — except you'll feel a whole lot better wearing one of these rib-tickling tees! "You Can't Spell Neurotic Without Erotic"; "Don't Come Near Me, I'm Acting Out"; "Anal Retentive And Looking To Clean!"; "These Aren't My Boobs — I'm Projecting"; "Warning! Repressed Memories Bubbling Up!"; "Sure I'm Over Forty, But Emotionally I'm Still Eight"; and, for the kids, "My Parents Went Into Therapy And All I Got Was This Lousy T-Shirt." PLUS a limited selection of Dr. Katz Bumper Stickers: "My Other Car Is My Therapist's Couch"; "I Brake For Passive-Aggressives"; "If I'm Huddled In A Corner Rocking, Don't Come A-Knocking"; more.

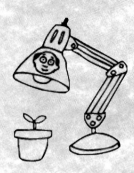

Dr. Katz's Mood Elevating/Growmatic Light System — Research shows that some people get those "winter blues" simply because they're not getting enough sunlight. Now you can banish that "twilight zone syndrome" forever! Dr. K's Mood Elevating/Growmatic Light System <u>looks</u> like an inexpensive table lamp — but it's more, much more! Plug it in, turn it on, treat yourself to simulated solar light (I call them "happy rays") — <u>and</u> grow common houseplants no matter what time of year it is! Hello, blue skies! Hello, green thumb!

Dr. Katz's All-Occasion Greeting Cards — Everyone loves greeting cards, but <u>these</u> greeting cards come with a little something extra: a few well-chosen words that say you're going to be all right. Beautiful, sensitive nature photography on the outside. On the inside, a variety of positive messages: "I Forgive You For Ruining My Childhood"; "I've Found The Source Of My Problem — Tag! You're It!"; "Thanks For Not Destroying Me The Way You Did My Mother/Father"; "I No Longer Wish You Were Dead"; "I've Come to Terms But I'm Not Coming to Thanksgiving"; more.

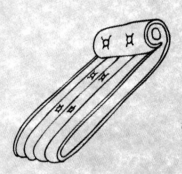

Dr. Katz Insta-Couch Air Mattress — Now you can be on the road and <u>really</u> be "on the road" — to emotional well-being! With the Dr. Katz Insta-Couch Air Mattress in your car trunk or airline bag, you've got a comfortable, therapist-grade couch to recline on and ponder your feelings anytime, anywhere! Don't miss those self-analysis sessions just because you promised to take the family to the Grand Canyon this year! The Dr. Katz Insta-Couch Air Mattress lets you explore new places and still explore the most fascinating place of all — Planet You.

Dad, are these great ideas or what?

I have to vote for "what." And I thought we discussed this videotape fantasy.

Hello! As part of my ongoing effort to provide you with the best therapy possible, I have devised the following Patient's Evaluation Form. Won't you take a few moments to fill it out at your convenience and drop it in the box in our reception area? This is an anonymous evaluation, so please <u>do not</u> write your name on the form. In addition, please don't ask Laura, my receptionist, to take the form from you. She has recently informed me of a skin condition that prevents her from handling paper.

1. How do you feel your therapy is progressing?

   I'm happy if you are. But I'd be happier if things were moving more quickly.

2. Do you feel that we are covering areas of importance?

   Definitely. But there's so much more I want to tell you.

3. After a typical session, do you feel hope, despair, or other emotion(s)?

   Gratitude. You are a special person.

4. What is the best thing about your therapy?

   Anticipation. As soon as I leave your office, I start thinking about our next time.

5. What is the worst thing about your therapy?

   Forty-five minutes isn't enough time with you. Oh, for an entire weekend!

6. If you could change one thing about our sessions, what would it be? I'd have them take place in the evening, in a quiet little restaurant. A candle on the table would suffuse our booth with a warm glow. There'd be a bottle of wine to help the conversation flow. And touching would definitely be allowed.

7. Are there any areas in which you think I, as your therapist, could improve?

   Relax your guard once in a while, Jonathan. Let your defenses down.

8. If I told you that I had written a self-help book, do you think you'd be tempted to purchase it?   Dozens! I'd give copies away as gifts.

9. Do you enjoy fresh, hot coffee?   Afterwards.

10. Please use the space below for any additional comments you'd like to make.

    You believe there's a line between doctor and patient that it would be unethical to cross. I respect that, Jonathan, I really do. But I can make my own decisions. And we're not getting any younger. I can always find another therapist. I'll <u>never</u> find another Jonathan!

6

Does this look like a woman's handwriting?

Dr. K.,
Here's that list. My friends don't have to make lists
when they want raises. By the way, I'm going to be in
late Monday. I have a doctor's appointment.
  L.

Why I Need A Raise

The patients have been asking me things again.

I have to think about the future.

I'm in a wedding in May and I have to pay for my own
dress even though it's lavender and you wouldn't wear
it again to a dog's funeral. There'll probably be a
shower too.

Inflation or something.

They had that citrus freeze or whatever in Florida
and the price of citruses went up.

My girlfriends all have company stock plans where
they can buy stock in the company. Why don't we
have that?

That memo you wrote me that time.

What if you get hit by a car? Where's my job security
then?

That time I had to talk to those Jehovah's Witnesses.

Your son Benjamin.

Session Notes 8/30

Patient: William Z.

Bill came to session direct from surgery (he'd washed up, but missed a spray of red dots above breast pocket. Blood? Couldn't stop staring at it). He complained once again about plastic surgeons' image. i.e., "pseudo-doctors, only in it for the money." Bill: "What about all the times we charter planes to Third World to do reconstructive work for free?" Me: "Very commendable work. How does it feel to do it?" Bill: "Never actually gone on one of those trips, but planning to when my practice slacks off a bit."

Bill very excited about new idea: adjustable breast implants. Borrowed my pad, sketched mini-inflation system: hollow rubber implants, series of tubes and valves, plus small CO_2 canister worn inside the brassiere. Bill: "You turn a switch and adjust the size of your breasts to suit the occasion. Let's say you're out for your morning jog, or just trying to ride a crowded subway comfortably. You move the switch to 'Small,' and ssssss, you're Audrey Hepburn. You get to work, release some CO_2 and you're a Medium: comfortable with your femininity, but not trading on it. Then after work you've got a date, so you slip into the ladies room, move the switch to 'Large,' and va-va-voom! You're Anna Nicole Smith. And if God forbid you're ever on a jetliner that has to ditch over the ocean, that 'Large' setting could save your life. It's all about flotation, Jonathan."

I resisted urge to say it's really all about avoidance. Wondered to myself what would happen if a valve ever got stuck and only one breast was working. Asked Bill if he wasn't dodging the real issue worrying him. Bill: "You're right. It's the issue of these incredible fees you charge." Polite laugh, ha ha. He makes more on one chubby liposuction patient than I could treating an airport full of agoraphobics for a year. Then he kept pushing it. "Seriously, Jonathan, I don't know why we don't figure out some kind of professional courtesy thing. You work on my problem, I do something

about the bags under your eyes. And is that a little jowly-wowly I see developing there?"

Could really learn to hate Bill, but I'm a professional. Saw my opening — pressed on. Me: "And what exactly is your problem?" He hemmed, hawed, said, "Oh, you know." I told him I wanted to hear him say it. Finally he looked at shoes and said, "It's Amanda, Jonathan. You know that." I said, "And who is Amanda, Bill? Please tell me who she is. It's important to verbalize this." He shook his head, said, "Amanda is a beautiful little mallard duck. She lives on the pond behind my country house. And I love her."

I felt this was significant progress — Bill finally ready to talk! Unfortunately time was up so I had to hustle him out, but tried to be encouraging while prodding him toward door. Just had time to check mirror before Mrs. J. arrived. There's no "jowly-wowly" there.

Hey Dad! Remember that idea we discussed about your own line of designer ~~rorscharsh~~ ~~roshchaurtz~~ ~~rosh hashona~~ inkblots for people to use when they watch your videotape? What's your opinion of these? I think I'm off to a great start here!

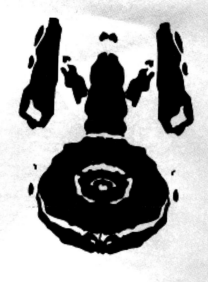

Potential Jobs for Ben

Job	Pro	Con
Middle management	Likes to supervise	Dislikes being supervised
Stockbroker	Enjoys handling others' money	Indictment virtually inevitable
Attorney	Will argue any topic	Requires study
Marketing consultant	No definable skills needed	Requires working
Newscaster	Already owns hair dryer	Cannot simulate concern for others
Therapist	Could benefit from my reputation	Could ruin my reputation
Auto mechanic	Could lie down on that little cart— likes to lie down	Would have to get up sometime
School crossing guard	Knows green from red	Questionable career track
Big Brother	Would teach him responsibility	Ben as role model?
Dog Walker	Likes dogs	Dogs dislike him
House-sitter	Solid track record of living in others' homes	Difficult to dislodge
Puppeteer	Has lively imagination	Too involved with hand already
Efficiency expert	Never wastes energy	I'm apparently cracking up

"The King"
(Chess Piece Shown Way Bigger Than Actual Size)

American Classic Collectibles
Presents
History's Greatest Therapists — The Chess Set

Now, the chess set that you have dreamed about has become a reality!

What therapist hasn't wished he or she could spend time with the giants of his or her field? Now he or she can! American Classic Collectibles has gathered all of history's greatest figures in psychiatry and psychology and fashioned them into 32 statuettes of gleaming Pewterex™* — a full regulation Chess Set. History's Greatest Therapists — The Chess Set features giants like Adler, Jung, Reich. Intriguing contemporary figures like Werner Erhard, Jeffrey Masson and Bob Newhart. And The Pawns — eight whimsical "patients," beautifully realized caricatures including The Whiner, The Cryer, The Kvetcher, The Blamer, The Denyer, The Binger, The Seether and The Doormat, "individuals" you're sure to recognize from your own practice! And of course, standing tall at a full four inches, The King and Queen — Sigmund and Anna Freud.

Finally, a chess set that tells the world that you're proud of who you are and what you do. History's Greatest Therapists — The Chess Set. Purchasing couldn't be easier. Simply return the enclosed order form with your credit card information or check for $59.95, and we will send you King Sigmund to examine in the comfort of your own home. If after ten days you don't agree that the workmanship, materials and design are clearly above average for a product of this type in a price range such as this, simply return it for a free refund. If you're as delighted with King Sigmund as we believe you will be, do nothing. Every three weeks you'll receive another piece and another invoice. With your last piece, we'll send you the Deluxe Woodtex™ Chess Board, a handsome complement to your chess set, and the complete History's Greatest Therapists will grace your mantle, coffee table or display case — for you to display, admire, and do battle with as you see fit. Start collecting today!

Attention canny investors in fine art: No one can predict how the market in Collectible Chess Sets will fare in the coming years. But American Classic Collectibles' Great Pontiffs Chess Set, issued in 1985, has already gone up 1 percent in value. The Semiautomatic Weaponry from Around the World Chess Set has gone up a solid 2 percent in value since its issue in 1989. And the Sylvester Stallone's Greatest Comedy Roles Chess Set has not lost more than 15 percent of its value (and most of that loss occurred the week they released *Oscar*). History's Greatest Therapists — The Chess Set, a strictly limited edition, will be manufactured and offered for sale for a period of one year. After 100,000 sets are produced, the molds will be destroyed and no more sets may ever be made. History's Greatest Therapists — The Chess Set is sure to become a classic among fairly discerning collectors everywhere.

*What is Pewterex™? A space-age metallic alloy with the look and heft of real pewter, fabricated at a fraction of pewter's cost. The savings are passed on to you! And Pewterex™ is the perfect complement to your Woodtex™ chessboard!

BeN & JONNY'S TAHITIAN TIKI BaR

Welcome to Ben and Jonny's, where the drinks are flaming and the customers cool! We know what "ales" ya, so sit back and relax while we "brew" up some fun. Oo-ah! Oo-ah! Volcano God want Fuzzy Navel!

Tonight's Specialty Concoctions!

LOA EXPECTATIONS. The perfect mix of curacao, peach liqueur, and oven-warmed gin. Nothing exotic about that combo, you say? Maybe not — unless you carbonate it like we have!

LAVA COME BACK. Who says Scotch and Canadian don't mix? You want blended whiskey, we've got your damn blended whiskey!

POLYNESIAN SCHNAPPSFEST. You take your peppermint schnapps, your apricot schnapps, your licorice schnapps, and an eyedroper full of children's antihistamine. You shake 'em up good and pour the whole blessed mess over ice. What makes it Polynesian? The pineapple wedge, silly!

RUM-BULL IN THE JUNGLE.
Jamaican Rum and good old
American malt liquor —that's your
Rum-Bull, my friend! The jungle?
Why, just look around you!

**BARE-BREASTED NATIVE
WOMEN.** With a name this good, we
could pour in any old crap we like
—and we do!

— And, as always —

750,000 **BEERS FROM AROUND THE WORLD.** With this many beers,
you'd expect some duplication — but at Ben and Jonny's? No way! We
wanted to make it an even million, but we gotta save _some_ room in the
back for ice!!!!

Don't forget your BEN AND JONNY'S T-Shirt, Baseball Cap.
Keychain and/or Beer Can Huggie! Oo-ah! Oo-ah! Volcano God say,
Pick Designated Driver and Get Home Safe!

Ben and Jonny's??? Volcano God????

Dear Mrs. Boyle,

I'd like to thank you for the opportunity to meet Joy. She has a wonderful personality, full of enthusiasm for life, and I thoroughly enjoyed our time together — even though that appointment was reserved for you, and, strictly speaking, bringing Joy along unannounced was an office "no-no."

Despite my positive impression of Joy, however, I'm afraid the meeting did nothing to change my mind. I still do not think it would be a good idea to accept her as a patient.

Please understand that I do not underestimate the seriousness of incontinence. I am well aware that it is nothing to be sniffed at. It can be a humiliating and debilitating condition for any human being, child or adult. But I'm not sure that what Joy has _is_ incontinence. It seems to me that she just may never have been properly housebroken. Might it be that you could solve her "problem" on your own, in a few simple sessions involving newspaper and yummy little treats? As for Joy's "other problem" — an unwillingess to heel — I can't even find that in any of my reference works, except for a few possibly related remarks under "Marriage."

In any case, I suggest you put Joy in the hands of a competent obedience expert. I am simply not equipped to treat her. Mrs. Boyle, it may not be "by the book," but I try very hard to like my patients. It would go against both my training and my instincts to make one of them wear a choke collar, or to push her nose repeatedly into her "messes" and call her a bad girl. And if my other patients were to find out about it, I can only imagine what their reactions would be (although I can think of at least two who would probably request the same treatment).

I hope you understand my position. I wish you luck with Joy. I hope that she finds some measure of contentment, and that her coat remains rich and lustrous. But I don't think I can treat her.

I'll see you, and you alone, next week. Please do not bring your tropical fish with you. I'm afraid there's not much I can do for them, either. (Frankly, I doubt that fish can exhibit signs of depression that you've described... although if I were a fish, I suppose I'd be pretty depressed about it myself.)

Sincerely,

Jonathan Katz, M.D.

HAGER, WALD, PERETTI, JOHNSON
ATTORNEYS AT LAW

Doctor Jonathan Katz
1124 North Sanchez Avenue

Dear Jonathan:

On behalf of Hager, Wald, Peretti, Johnson, I'd like to thank you again for taking the time and trouble to serve as expert witness in the case of the *State* vs. *Andrew Fierst*. The testimony of expert witnesses has become a linchpin of the American legal system, thanks to conscientious professionals like yourself.

All of us here at Hager, Wald agreed that for a courtroom novice, you did a fine job. As promised, I've dashed off a few tips on how you can make your next court appearance go even more smoothly. Please take them in the constructive spirit in which they are offered.

1. REMEMBER WHERE YOU ARE. I know that force of habit is a tough thing to shake. When you are asked to testify in your capacity as a professional, the natural inclination is to behave as you would at your own place of business. Or maybe you were just nervous, I don't know. But the jury was very confused when the district attorney was questioning you and you stood up, walked to the back of the courtroom and peeked out the door to see if your next patient had arrived yet.

2. COURTROOM INTERRUPTIONS ARE NOT TAKEN LIGHTLY. I know this was not your fault, Jonathan, and I'm sure you've probably already taken steps to assure that it never happens again. But having a witness's testimony interrupted when his son bursts into court, makes his way up to the stand and asks for the car keys is unprecedented in American jurisprudence. By the way, doesn't your son work?

3. STICK TO THE SUBJECT AT HAND. It probably puts your patients at ease when you tell them a little story or anecdote to illustrate a point. But the court system is clogged enough as it is without bizarre digressions adding to the delays. I'm sure some of the jurors are <u>still</u> trying to figure out what the fable of the ant and the grasshopper had to do with a purse-snatching case.

4. NEVER PROVOKE THE JUDGE. You'll recall that the judge said he was having trouble following one specific part of your testimony. Your response was, "And what kind of emotions does that stir up? Does it trigger a sense of inadequacy or frustration?" Probably nothing more than a therapist's reflex response, but it really ticked him off. You probably realized this yourself when he cited you for contempt of court.

On the plus side, Jonathan, I think you made a very credible witness (until your son showed up). You were polite, well dressed, well spoken and knowledgeable about your field of expertise. I'm sure you'll be called again to serve as an expert witness, and I'm sure that next time you'll avoid the little peccadillos you committed this time. And as I told you the day of closing arguments, it's not necessarily a reflection on the witness's testimony when both the prosecutor and the defense ask the jury to disregard it. It's just old-fashioned legal wrangling.

Sincerely,

Gregory Lavides, Esq.
Hager, Wald, Peretti, Johnson
Attorneys at Law
gl:rf

cc: Mr. Andrew Fierst
County Men's Correctional Facility

Session Notes 6/3

Patient: Tony L.

Session began with what's become a mini-ritual. Thanked Tony for latest drawings of me. He asked if I liked them. I said yes, was flattered. He asked if I really liked them. Me: yes, very much. Tony: more than the last batch, and if so, why'd I lie to him about liking last batch? Me: hadn't compared the two sets of drawings, didn't intend to. Saw my opening to start the session, said: in the arts as in life, it's difficult to quantify worth — how rate one drawing, or dance, or song "better" than another? Accept them all as expressions of humanity. Tony seemed to be listening. I pressed on, saying I could no more judge which drawing was best than he could judge which parent loved him more, or which sibling got "best" attention when growing up. Urged him to lay these questions to rest, turn his energy toward his art. Tony, nodding eagerly: "Yeah, so what are you telling me, the drawings stink?" Suddenly remembered I'd forgotten to buy Tylenol.

Tony said again I remind him physically of his father.

Annoyed me — he's eight years older than me, just happens to have a teenager's hairline. Annoyance unprofessional, so I simply smiled, let moment pass. Tony: "Yeah, I guess it's that whole Superdome look. The huge expanse of flesh above the eyebrows. The Kojak thing. You're not self-conscious about being virtually hairless, are you, Doc?" I replied I was comfortable with normal signs of aging. Then asked him whether any new progress

with his prostate. Mistake. Tony's eyes filled with tears. Tony: "I loved my father, Dr. Katz. Damn it, I loved that man!" Then excused himself to urinate.

Tony better after visit to bathroom. He may have caught me rummaging desk drawer for Tylenol. Not sure. Maybe slammed it shut in time. Session ended amicably, Tony promising new batch of drawings this week. Alone in office, I counted slowly to 100 before buzzing Laura. Me: "Know of a pharmacy that delivers?" Laura: "Try the Yellow Pages."

AAAAA

TRACKING, PROCESS SERVING
AND REPOSSESSION SERVICES

"Serving the legal and financial communities since 1986"

Dear Client:

Following is (are) the address(es) and phone number(s) of the individual(s) whose whereabouts you requested. Please note that our invoice is payable upon receipt. Should you require further assistance, do not hesitate to call AAAAA TRACKING, PROCESS SERVING AND REPOSSESSION SERVICES.

Thank you for your patronage.

Jody H.: Married, stayed local. Husband: corporate exec, full, thick hair (she <u>claims</u>). Moderate weight gain. Two children. Remembers going to see "2001" junior year, does not remember eating hash brownies in theater.

Amelia G.: Divorced, West Coast. Ex-husband: Realtor, hair weave. No children. Moderate weight gain. Doesn't remember us dating but remembers my underarm perspiration stains in English. Did not pursue.

Betsy B.: Divorced, stayed local. Ex-husband: lumber wholesaler, thinning at crown. One child. Claims no weight gain. No interest in meeting (is currently lesbian).

Rose F.: Married, Florida. No further info available (uncooperative). Claims no memory of me but I think she's lying (why else would she threaten to call police?).

Janice R.: Divorced, Cleveland. Ex-husband: organic grocer, ponytail (she <u>claims</u>), under restraining order to stay away. Weight gain: "I've learned to be comfortable with who I am. The drugs help." Two children, whereabouts unknown. Often thinks of me and what might have been. Eager to meet, reconnect. I pleaded busy travel schedule.

This is disappointing. Try college dates next?

THE FIELDGATE SCHOOL
Est. 1885
Office of the Headmaster

Dear Dr. Katz,

Thank you so much for agreeing to speak at this year's Commencement ceremonies. It is always gratifying when our Speaker is someone who has personally benefited from the Fieldgate experience, and while your son Benjamin may not have been one of our most distinguished students academically, several of our instructors remember him as a well-liked child, within his small circle of friends.

Here are some particulars on The Fieldgate School's Commencement Day. Our Commencement ceremonies will begin with a reception promptly at

GOOD AFTERNOON, STUDENTS, ALUMNI, FAMILIES, DISTINGUISHED FACULTY AND MR. HEADMASTER. LOOKING AROUND AT ALL THESE HAPPY YOUNG FACES, I AM REMINDED OF MY OWN SOMEWHAT DIFFERENT EDUCATIONAL EXPERIENCE. I WENT TO A PUBLIC SCHOOL WITH A WELL-EARNED REPUTATION FOR TOUGHNESS. WHY, THE KIDS ON THE DEBATING TEAM TOOK STEROIDS! HA HA HA. I'M KIDDING, OF COURSE. JUST SAY NO. (WOULD THE JOKE ABOUT THE KANGAROO IN THE BAR BE BETTER?)

TODAY IS A DAY OF CELEBRATION AND JOY. FOR TODAY IS THE DAY WE GATHER TO HONOR THOSE STUDENTS — OUR SONS AND DAUGHTERS — WHO HAVE ACCEPTED THE CHALLENGE OF ONE OF OUR FINEST, MOST RIGOROUS INSTITUTIONS OF LEARNING — ACCEPTED *AND MET* THAT CHALLENGE. WE HONOR THOSE FIELDGATE STUDENTS TODAY IN THE SAME WAY THAT THOSE STUDENTS HAVE HONORED FIELDGATE BY THEIR ACHIEVEMENTS — INDEED, IN THE SAME WAY I CONSIDER *MYSELF* HONORED TO BE ASKED TO DELIVER THESE COMMENCEMENT REMARKS. THAT'S THREE KINDS OF HONOR GOING ON AT ONCE, AND I'VE JUST BEGUN TO SPEAK. BUT HONORED IS WHAT I AM. FOR IT HAS ALWAYS BEEN A DREAM OF MINE TO GIVE A GRADUATION ADDRESS AT A FINE INSTITUTION OF LEARNING, AND WHILE I PICTURED SOMETHING CLOSER TO THE UNIVERSITY LEVEL THAN A PRESCHOOL, I THINK WE ALL AGREE THAT EDUCATION IS EDUCATION — WHETHER IT INVOLVES CONQUERING QUANTUM PHYSICS, MAPPING NEW AREAS OF THE HUMAN BRAIN, OR LEARNING TO WIPE YOUR RUNNY NOSE ON A TISSUE INSTEAD OF ALL UP AND DOWN YOUR ARM.

I AM PARTICULARLY HONORED — THERE'S THAT WORD AGAIN (CHUCKLE HERE) — I AM PARTICULARLY HONORED TO BE YOUR SPEAKER BECAUSE MY OWN SON BENJAMIN IS A FIELDGATE ALUMNUS. IT SEEMS LIKE AGES AGO THAT BEN'S MOTHER AND MYSELF WHEELED HIM UP FIELDGATE'S MAJESTIC FRONT WALK, DODGED AN ERRANT SOCCER BALL WHOSE UNAUTHORIZED FLIGHT WAS TESTIMONY TO THE HIGH SPIRITS AND APPRECIATION OF ATHLETICS TO BE FOUND WITHIN THESE

HALLOWED HALLS, AND BEGAN WHAT WE FONDLY REMEMBER (BEN
AND I, THAT IS. I CAN'T SPEAK FOR HIS MOTHER) AS OUR
"FIELDGATE EXPERIENCE." I RECALL ONLY TOO WELL — AS I'M
SURE YOU ALL DO! — THE BARRAGE OF TESTS AND INTERVIEWS BEN
WAS SUBJECTED TO. I REALIZE NOW THAT THEY WERE DESIGNED
ONLY TO ASSURE THAT HE WOULD BENEFIT COMPLETELY FROM LIFE
AT FIELDGATE, BUT AT THE TIME, IT SEEMED LIKE THE
INSTRUCTORS WERE EXPECTING RATHER A LOT FROM A THREE-
YEAR-OLD. "WHICH BUNNY IS HAPPY, BENJAMIN? WHICH BUNNY IS
SAD?" "DO YOU KNOW WHICH OF THESE SHAPES IS A CIRCLE,
BENJAMIN? NO, NOT THAT ONE, BUT THAT'S A GOOD GUESS."
(CHUCKLE HERE) "YOU LOOK UNCOMFORTABLE, BENJAMIN. DO YOU
NEED TO USE THE POTTY? DO YOU KNOW *HOW* TO USE THE POTTY?"

AND THEN, JUST WHEN I THOUGHT BEN HAD SQUEAKED THROUGH,
THERE WERE THE QUESTIONS FOR ME: IS HE COMFORTABLE IN
GROUPS? DOES HE REQUIRE A MID-MORNING NAP? WILL YOU BE
REQUESTING FINANCIAL AID? I'LL BE CANDID: AT THE TIME I
THOUGHT TO MYSELF, "IF YOUR ADMISSION STANDARDS ARE SO
RIGOROUS, WHY CAN'T YOUR STUDENTS WORK THE WATER FOUNTAIN
WITHOUT HELP?" (WINK HERE IF IT FEELS RIGHT) FRANKLY, I
WASN'T SURE BEN WAS READY FOR SCHOOL AT ALL, BUT HIS
MOTHER SAID THAT SHE HAD PUT IN THREE YEARS OF SLAVERY,
ENDURING MORE THAN ANY INTELLIGENT ADULT SHOULD BE
EXPECTED TO, AND THAT THIS ILL-CONSIDERED DECISION TO
HAVE A CHILD HAD ALREADY CAUSED IRREPARABLE DAMAGE TO HER
CAREER, TO SAY NOTHING OF HER BREASTS. HOWEVER, I DO NOT
WISH TO WANDER AFIELD FROM MY CHOSEN TOPIC. AND THAT TOPIC
IS FIELDGATE — WHAT IT STANDS FOR, AND WHAT IT HAS MEANT
TO BEN AND MYSELF. IF I MAY BE SERIOUS FOR A MOMENT: I
BELIEVE THAT WHATEVER DISCIPLINE, WHATEVER DILIGENCE BEN
DISPLAYS — WHATEVER HE HAS ABSORBED OF WHAT USED TO BE
CALLED THE AMERICAN WORK ETHIC — BEGAN RIGHT HERE AT
FIELDGATE. IN FACT, I WISH BEN WERE HERE WITH ME THIS
AFTERNOON SO I COULD SHOW YOU HOW A "FIELDGATE CHILD"
DEVELOPS INTO A "FIELDGATE MAN OR WOMAN," BUT HE WAS
UNAVOIDABLY DETAINED ON OUT-OF-TOWN BUSINESS DUE TO A
SCHEDULING MIXUP. (LOOK DISAPPOINTED) NEVERTHELESS, BEN
HIMSELF WOULD BE THE FIRST TO TELL YOU THAT

FROM THE SKETCHPAD OF TONY LANG
Fine Art/Commercial Art/Rustproofing

Hey Doc, You know that bizarro things occur to me when I'm working — it's all part of letting the imagination run free, I guess! — and I was in my studio, putting the finishing touches on a canvas and thinking about our last session and how rewarding it was, when it hit me: how lucky we are in our modern age to have professional therapists, and what a shame it is that people like yourself weren't available to folks in earlier centuries. Or maybe not — I mean, what if you'd convinced Columbus that wanting to sail to America was just an immature urge brought on by fear of commitment? Doc, pick a century, any century — you could have done a lot of damage!

Dr. Katz the Great

Dr. Katz XIV

Ha ha ha, you know when I'm needling you. I'm a huge fan, Doc, I don't have to tell you that. Heck, you gotta admire a guy who's convinced so many people to pay him just to sit there and pretend he's listening. People who work a hell of a lot harder than you do, Doc! Ha ha ha!! I'm joking.

The point is — ol' Doodling Tony made an appearance that day, and I thought you might get a kick out of the results. Let me know if you do!

Thanks for being my friend! See you next time. Tony

P.S. By the way, loved you on that radio show. The urine jar guy was a scream!!!

Queen Dr. Katz the First

Dr. Katz Professional Father of Our Country

"JOHNNY TALLTREE, MINING MAN"
By J. Katz, Professional Therapist

(Stirring tempo, flatpick strum)

Johnny Talltree, Mining Man
His story now I sing
Hamm'rin' with his pick and axe
He'd make those mineshafts ring, my boys,
He'd make those mineshafts ring.
Old Johnny knew his glinting ore
His pyrite from his gold
And when he set that pick to rock
He'd hammer hard and bold, my boys,
He'd hammer hard and bold.

Now Johnny was a-hamm'rin' hard
When the pit boss Jake McQueen
Said, "Gather round and weep before
The new minin' machine, my boys,
The new minin' machine."
She was tall and stout and gleamed all o'er,
Her pistons straight and true,
"She'll outwork ten of you," said Jake,
She'll outwork ten of you."
Now Johnny, he looked o'er the machine
And he knew 'twas built to last,
But a miner's pride is a powerful thing,
Old John said, "Not so fast, my boys,"
Old John said "Not so fast."
The machine was put in Shaft Thirteen
In Twelve was our lad John,
Jake McQueen said, "Let 'em go!"
And the mining race was on, my boys,
The mining race was on.

Those mighty pistons strained and strained
John's pick'd lift and fall,
The mineshafts shuddered with the blows
And the piles of ore grew tall, my boys,
The piles of ore grew tall.
Now Johnny fought the valiant fight
But a man is but a man,
Old Johnny lost his footing, and
He fell right on his can, my boys,
He fell right on his can.
Old Jake McQueen, he sneered at John,
"I guess you're out of steam."
When they heard a mighty cracking sound
The machine had hit a beam, my boys,
The machine had hit a beam.

The shaft was shaking, rocks poured down,
The men they ran like hell,
But a timber hit old Jake McQueen
And trapped him where he fell, my boys,
It trapped him where he fell.
The machine, it sputtered, shuddered, stopped,
Completely out of gas,
John knew he'd have to save old Jake,
So he got up off his ass, my boys,
He got up off his ass.

Now Johnny hammered, Johnny hauled,
And Johnny got Jake free
The boss's life was saved that day
By Mine Man John Talltree, my boys,
By Mine Man John Talltree.
Well the comp'ny downsized everyone
Said the payroll'd got too big,
Old Jake retrained for M.I.S.,
But a mine man's gotta dig, my boys,
A mine man's gotta dig.
So Johnny took his buyout pay
Retired to Palm Springs
Got a floppy hat 'n' one of those
Metal detector things, my boys,
Metal detector things.
Now Johnny spends his quiet days
Sweepin' the desert sands
He holds that metal detector thing
In pow'rful miner's hands, my boys,
In pow'rful miner's hands.

Sometimes he finds a coin or two
Sometimes a broken watch,
Once he found a statuette
Of a hula dancer's crotch, my boys,
A hula dancer's crotch.
And he never talks of who he is
Or what he did that day,
But away back east in mine country,
You sometimes hear them say, my boys,
You sometimes hear them say:
"On this spot man took on machine,
It happened just in here,
And the man was looking pretty good,
'Til he fell right on his rear, my boys,
'Til he fell right on his rear."

(Slow way down, one more time, dramatically:)

"'Til he fell right on his rear."

This may be the best song I've ever written! Play
for the rest of the Katz and Jammers A.S.A.P.

TO

TIME ▼	
7	15
	30
	45
8	15
	30
	45
9	15
	30
	45
10	15
	30
	45
11	15
	30
	45
12	15
	30
	45
1	15
	30
	45
2	15
	30
	45
3	15
	30
	45
4	15
	30
	45
5	15
	30
	45
6	15
	30
	45

7

8

3

4

5

6

TIME ▼

7

8

Dark images of seething fury.
Tony Lang
"Fifty Ways to Kill Your Therapist"
Sketches, oils, sculpture
Through March 4th
Gallery Violentique
Avenue E

PLACE
STAMP
HERE

Dr. K. —Hope you can come!
Tony

Dr. Jonathan Katz
Professional Therapist
Please Hand Deliver

NOTE: If you are offended by images of brutality or by displays of animal viscera, you may not find this exhibition enjoyable.

2

3

4

5

6

What My Father Does For A Living
By Benjamin Katz

What my father does for a living is hes a therapist. That means he helps people feel better when the'yre sad or angry. They come to his office and talk and he sits there and nods and then he tells them it sounds like the'yve got good reason to feel the way they do and that makes them get happy and go away. I know this from hiding in his closet one day and listening. I heard one man came in and he said he was suffering from importance, and they talked a lot about it and my dad said "this happens to everyone at one time or another" and the man said "not to Barry the Jackhammer Walsh it doesnt happen!" and he stormed off and I don't know what's so bad about being important anyway. most people would want to be important if you ask me. but when I asked my father about this later he got very upset and figured out what I'd done and thats when he decided to move his practice out of our apartment and get an office. Well, it wasn't him really who decided so much, it was more my mom. By the way she wants to know why this essay doesn't ask What My Mother Does For A Living and who are you, Mrs. Idoni to just assume she sits around baking cookies and using lemon freshner on the laundry. Which I guess is a good question since she certainly doesnt do those things. She said I should tell you a womans place is in the house and the senate and then she laughed like this weird laugh. Mom sure gets mad a lot these days.

Anyway you know whats a real pain in the neck about my dads job is he doesn't work with heavy machinery or drive a truck or an airplane or guard dangerous criminals or anything. he just sits around listening. so theres really nothing fun about it for a kid. Plus if I go to him with a problem or something I never know whos listening — is it Dad or is it Dr. Dad, Profesional Therapist? Like I busted the head off one of my G.I. Joes and showed it to him and instead of fixing it he looked at it and said, "How does that make you feel?" I said "It makes me feel like someone should fix it. Hello in there, is anybody home?" I picked up that last phrase from Mom, she says it to him a lot. I didn't show the G.I. Joe to her because she'll just get started about war toys and next thing you know Im enrolled in another one of those Saturday morning crafts classes with the potholders. Yecch.

Anyway that is what My Father Does For A Living. I believe Ive learned a lot from watching my dad about how exciting and rewarding working can be. When I grow up I plan to inherit money.

THOUGHT
The Publication That Ponders

Dr. Jonathan Katz
1124 N. Sanchez Avenue

Dear Dr. Katz:

The Submissions Review Committee of THOUGHT, The Publication That Ponders, is pleased to inform you that we have read your proposal for an article titled "Were Aristotle and Plato Codependent?" with much interest and enthusiasm. We would like to commission the complete article for publication in our next available issue.

We have enclosed some simple writer's guidelines to bear in mind when composing your article. Our most important guideline, of course, is that your work must demonstrate the sort of intellectual liveliness, meticulous research and aversion to cliched, conventional thought that our readers demand.

We have also included a return envelope for use in submitting your manuscript and a small processing fee to THOUGHT. As you know, a journal such as ours, engaged in the loftier realms of reflection and debate, cannot survive without the generosity not only of its readers but its contributors. When submitting your article, please include a check to cover pre-publication processing costs at the rate of 25 cents per word. If the length of your article exceeds 10,000 words, please increase that figure to 40 cents per word. We apologize for the higher rate, but lengthier articles require us to retain the services of an editor.

Additionally, it would save our accounting department a lot of "red tape" if you would be so kind as to make the check out to Cash.

Welcome to the family of THOUGHT! We look forward to reading your article!

Yours in intellectual liveliness,

Conor P. Royston, Ph.D.
Publisher
THOUGHT

Hello! As part of my ongoing effort to provide you with the best therapy possible, I have devised the following Patient's Evaluation Form. Won't you take a few moments to fill it out at your convenience and drop it in the box in our reception area? This is an anonymous evaluation, so please do not write your name on the form. In addition, please don't ask Laura, my receptionist, to take the form from you. She has recently informed me of a skin condition that prevents her from handling paper.

1. How do you feel your therapy is progressing?

   Not so good. I continue to have that dream about eating human flesh.

2. Do you feel that we are covering areas of importance?

   Each time the dream gets a little more vivid. I'm afraid one day its going to come true.

3. After a typical session, do you feel hope, despair, or other emotion(s)?

   Well, who am I kidding? I'm sure its going to come true. I'm scared to death, Doctor, and you're not doing anything about it.

4. What is the best thing about your therapy? Do you know that I've removed all the condiments from my kitchen, because I'm afraid one day my husband will come in and I'll be seized by the urge to sprinkle salt and pepper on him and take a nice juicy bite?

5. What is the worst thing about your therapy?

   Ironic, isn't it, when I otherwise find him so physically repulsive?

6. If you could change one thing about our sessions, what would it be?

   I think he suspects something. Last week I woke up with a big scrap of pillowcase in my mouth. I told him it must have got caught in my bridgework.

7. Are there any areas in which you think I, as your therapist, could improve?

   Why won't you help me with this? Why can't you see that its eating me up (no pun intended)? Why do you act as if its not happening.

8. If I told you that I had written a self-help book, do you think you'd be tempted to purchase it? Is it because I haven't told you about the dream? Is that why? Yes, I'll bet that's it.

9. Do you enjoy fresh, hot coffee?

   I do like a nice cup of coffee. It gives me that little "oomph" I need to get going.

10. Please use the space below for any additional comments you'd like to make.

    Help me, Doctor, help me!

    Rethink this whole evaluation form idea?

Thera-Date

"Someone special needs your attention"

Satisfied single therapists nationwide know...
DATING IS THE BEST THERAPY!

Dear Fellow Professional Therapist,

Does this story sound familiar to you?

> "I couldn't understand it. I was fit and attractive. I had a thriving practice, making good money helping people. I had made it possible for my patients to enter healthy relationships, but I didn't seem to have the time, the energy or the luck to find someone special for myself."

You know what a special person you are. Your patients know. But how is Mr. or Ms. Right supposed to find out?

Thera-Date, that's how. Thera-Date is the *only* computer-match dating service *expressly* created for and tailored to the professional therapists' community. Unlike other dating services which treat everyone "alike," Thera-Date's exclusive companion-link procedures take *full account* of the fact that *therapists are very special people* — who deserve to *meet* very special people. That's why Thera-Date has the endorsement of leading therapists' organizations* — and why Thera-Date is the right dating service for *you.*

Joining Thera-Date is as easy as falling off your office couch! Just fill in the following brief questionnaire.

1. What is your marital status? ☐ single ☐ divorced ☐ widowed ☐ legally separated
☐ had spouse declared incompetent

2. Are you new to the area? ☐ yes ☐ no
If yes, where are you from? _____
If yes, did you relocate following a malpractice suit? ☐ yes ☐ no
If yes, did you change your name afterward? ☐ yes ☐ no

3. Do you live alone? ☐ yes ☐ no
With a roommate? ☐ yes ☐ no
With a stranger or strangers? ☐ yes ☐ no
Do you have children living with you? ☐ yes ☐ no If yes, ages _____
Are these children yours or someone else's? ☐ mine ☐ someone else's
If someone else's, what are you, some kind of sicko? ☐ yes ☐ no

Formal training in therapy: ☐ Bachelor's degree ☐ Master's degree ☐ Doctorate ☐ M.D.
☐ Aerobics instructor's certificate

5. Are you currently employed as a therapist? ☐ yes ☐ no
If no, what is your current occupation?_____
If no, are you secretly treating patients in violation of a court order? ☐ yes ☐ oh, no

6. Which best describes your style of therapist-patient interaction?
- ☐ "I'm okay, you're okay."
- ☐ "I can help you — if you'll let me."
- ☐ "I know what's best for you."
- ☐ "I'm sorry, were you saying something?"

7. Income: ☐ under $25,000 ☐ $25,001–$50,000 ☐ $50,001–$100,000 ☐ $100,001–$500,000 ☐ real money

8. What are your relationship goals? ☐ casual dating ☐ long-term relationship ☐ marriage ☐ tear off a piece ☐ prove to my mother once and for all that I'm straight ☐ anything unindictable

9. Check the statement that best applies to you.
"According to the last person I dated, the relationship collapsed because..."
- ☐ I acted like an arrogant boor.
- ☐ I acted like a pompous ass.
- ☐ I acted like a supercilious snob.
- ☐ We drifted apart.

10. Which age group do you prefer dating? ☐ 18–25 ☐ 25–35 ☐ 35–45 ☐ 45 and above ☐ Have you read Nabokov?

11. Would you like to meet someone who has children? ☐ yes ☐ no ☐ if they're dead

12. What educational background do you prefer? ☐ high school ☐ college ☐ postgraduate ☐ Can write own name ☐ block letters ☐ cursive

13. Are you interested in someone who smokes? ☐ yes ☐ no ☐ smokes what? ☐ prefer someone who bursts into flame

14. What qualities are most important to you in a date (check all that apply)? ☐ intelligence ☐ attitude ☐ sense of humor ☐ political outlook ☐ social conscience ☐ breast size ☐ penile length ☐ breast size *and* penile length

15. What areas of interest would you like to share with someone?
☐ talking about myself ☐ thinking about myself ☐ getting in touch with my own feelings ☐ finally taking the time to get to know the real me ☐ snowboarding

16. Are you bothered by gross physical deformities? ☐ of course not ☐ not at all ☐ only in others

...And that's all there is to it! Don't delay — use the enclosed mailer to return the questionnaire and your check for $99.95, and you'll join the thousands of satisfied therapists who have "made a connection" through Thera-Date! Remember: If you're listening to someone and they're not paying you for it, they'd better be someone special! With Thera-Date, *they will be!!!*

*not including the American Psychological Association, the International Fellowship of Psychologists, the American College of Psychological Therapy, the National Therapists' Register, the United States Congress of Psychiatric Professionals, Who's Who Among American Psychologists and Psychiatrists, or any other nationally or locally accredited professional therapists' group. If you are not a professional therapist and this brochure has reached you by mistake, you may be interested in one of the following other services: Accountant-Date, Anesthesiolo-Date, Baptist-Date, Broker-Date, Chronic Yeast Infecto-Date, Cowboy-Date, Camel Trainer-Date, Diamond Merchant-Date, Elephantiasis Sufferer-Date, Embryonic Surgeon-Date, Farmer-Date, General-Date, Gout-Date, Halcion Addict-Date, Helicopter Pilot-Date, Hologram Artist-Date, Igloo Architect-Date, Jew-Date 2000, Koala-Date, Laryngecto-Date, Meter Man/Maid-Date, Minoxidil User-Date, Moslem-Date, Nasturtium Fancier-Date, Orgasm 2000, Priest-Date, Python Owner-Date, Quantum Physicist-Date, Randy Boys 2000, Reebok-Wearer Date, Sample Case Manufacturer-Date, Sophomoric Joke Teller-Date, Subtitle Proofreader-Date, Table Dancer-Date, Telemarketer-Date, Toaster Repairperson-Date, Tyrolean Hat Fancier-Date, Uvula Fetisher-Date, Volume Discount Store Operator-Date, Viola Aficionado-Date, Violent Spouse Abuser-Date, White Dates Only, Xerox Fluid Sniffer-Date, Yellowish Look Around the Eyes-Date, Yo Baby! The Dating Service for African Americans, Zamboni Driver-Date, Zoologi-Date, ZZZ! The Meeting Place for Narcoleptics.

Dr. K,
Can you do someThing abouT The way your recepTionisT chews her gum? Today she popped a bubble and I ThoughT I'd been shoT.

Dear Dr. Katz,
This suggestion box of yours is a good idea. I suggest you get a life.

Dr. Katz - You're not taking a week off again this summer, are you? I think that's very irresponsible.

DEAR DR. KATZ,

DOES THE I.R.S. ALLOW

YOU TO CLAIM

CODEPENDENTS?

Dear Dr. Katz ~
Why don't we ever talk about ~~your~~ mother?

Dr. K, You know that tie of yours with the blue and yellow strypes? There's been a little orange stain on it for about three years now. It's driving me crazy.

Dr. Katz,
Do you have any suggestions about which Psychic Hot Lines are better than others?

Dear Dr. Katz,
Why don't you give that nice girl who works for you a raise? She puts up with a lot from us annoying patients.

Dr. K, I think I've finally figured out the correct chronological order of my past lives!

TODAY

You used 2060
AMOUNT OF ELECTRICITY
reading (actual)
ding (KWH)

5 per KWH = 218.00
5 per KWH ÷

T YEAR
Average customer usage

your actual usag
BY BILLING MON

Elec
year 565 -
d: this year 56

HOW ABOUT SOME
NEW MAGAZINES IN THE
WAITING ROOM, KATZ?
I'M GETTING A LITTLE TIRED READING
ABOUT PRESIDENT EISENHOWER.

NO POSTAGE
NECESSARY
IF MAILED
IN THE
UNITED STATES

BUSINESS REPLY MAIL
FIRST CLASS MAIL PERMIT NO

DR. KATZ,
HOW CAN YOU INSIST THAT DREAMS HOLD
THE KEY TO THE SUBCONSCIOUS, THEN
REFUSE TO ADMIT THE POSSIBILITY
THAT THEY MIGHT ALSO HOLD THIS
WEEKS LOTTERY NUMBERS?
I CALL THAT HYPOCRISY.

Dr. Katz
Which personality disorders
do you think are the funniest?

Dr. K.,
You don't like
me very much,
do you?

Doctor Katz,
Do you EVER do
group therapy
night for singles?

WHAT THIS OFFICE NEEDS
IS A MINI BAR.
ACTUALLY, FULL ROOM SERVICE
WOULD BE EVEN BETTER.

DR. KATZ,
MY DENTIST PUT A TV IN HIS OFFICE SHOWING A
REALLY INTERESTING VIDEO ABOUT TOOTH
WHITENING. WHY DON'T YOU DO THAT?

Dr. Katz
Would you be interested
in my problems if I wasn't
paying you? How about you
stop billing me for a
while and we'll find
out?

SUN MON TUE WE

5

6

Dance the Night Away For a Good Cause at the
KATZ AND JAMMERS Annual Children's Fund Benefit

Assembly Hall
Saturday, August 14th
8:00 P.M.

Katz and Jammers "Prescription Folk, Rock and Blues"!

with

Dr. Jonathan Katz, Professional Therapist, vocals, guitar, harmonica
Dr. James "Jimmy Soul" Nelson, Orthodonture, vocals, lead guitar
Dr. Michele Kokinda, Dermatologist, vocals, keyboards
Dr. Wilfred "Tiny" Seaver, Cardiology, fiddle, banjo, guitar
Dr. Stanley Ochshorn, Podiatrist, Bass
Dr. Louis Donelli, Pediatrics, drums and percussion

Playing these Katz And Jammers favorites:
Lonesome Train Blues · Several Deep Breaths · Your Love's like a Booster Shot · Green Bunions · Tell Me About
Your Childhood · Teeth Don't Straighten on Their Own · Don't Be Afraid < Your Body's Changing > · Stress
Test of Your Love · Overbite and Underpaid · Johnny Talltree, Mining Man · Stiletto Heels < Hurt Your
Metatarsals > · I Want Your Body Fat · Nat'rally Oily Skin · Treadmill's Gettin' Faster and I'm Just Slowin
Down · Cherries in the Snow · Fallen Arches, Lord · Your Anger's Valid < But You Have to Let It Go > · L'il
Swedish Sedan · I'm Your Night Retainer

...and many others! The Doctors Are In at the KATZ AND JAMMERS
Annual Children's Fund Benefit! Be there!
Don't forget the Katz and Jammers' album, "Direct Reimbursement," on Vanitas CDs and tapes.

Hey, Dad, guess what? I wrote a song for the Katz and Jammers!

GOT 2 BE WHO I'M GONNA BE
BY DJ Ben Jammin'

(First verse:)
> Bad news when I walk through the hood of my youth
> All the people are illin' and bein' uncouth
> And The Man don't let nobody get ahead
> So 2day I'm just gonna stay in my bed
> See they tryin' 2 break me but I'm 2 cool
> I be thinkin' 'bout goin' back 2 graduate school
> Cause I'm feelin' broke down like a motherless child
> Chance of morning showers but continued mild

(Chorus:)
> Got 2 be who I'm gonna be
> Not a member of your society
> Shackled by responsibility
> Man, I can't find a thing on the damn TV

(Second verse:)
> When The Man say Son you got 2 get a job
> I say Man, that ain't nothin' but a license 2 rob
> You takin' money from people for the things you do
> Man, what them poor people ever do 2 you?
> Plus my expertise is in how I chill
> And The Man sayin' no way that's a marketable skill
> But it's what I do, and I know I'm the best
> Light starch on the shirts, and I'd like the pants pressed

(Chorus:)
> Got 2 be who I'm gonna be
> You say I'm no good? Well I disagree
> I'm proud of my people's history
> Prob'ly be home late but I have my key

(Third verse:)
> Break it down!
> Uh-huh
> Uh-huh
> Break it down y'all!

(Chorus:)
> Got 2 be who I'm gonna be
> I'm a menace 2 your society
> I went 4 a walk 2 the grocery
> 8 a sandwich and 1 the lottery
> Yeah, Got 2 be who I'm gonna be
> Got 2 wonder who really killed Kennedy
> If you ask a French guy if he has 2 pee
> It'd be pretty funny if he said "Oui Oui"
> Break it down!

Tell Ben we don't do rap. Try 2 be diplomatic.

AMES, AMES, URQUHART AND FIELDSMITH
ATTORNEYS-AT-LAW

Doctor Jonathan Katz
1124 North Sanchez Avenue

Dear Dr. Katz:

I would like to bring a matter to your attention on behalf of my client, Laura Silverstein. As you may know, Ms. Silverstein is currently employed as your receptionist.

Ms. Silverstein has informed me that she has lately become the object of unwanted attentions from a Benjamin Katz. As you are perhaps aware, Mr. Katz is (or claims to be) your son. According to my client, Mr. Katz enjoys virtually unlimited access to your reception area — puzzling, as yours is ostensibly a place of business and my client informs me that Mr. Katz is chronically unemployable. According to Ms. Silverstein, Mr. Katz invariably greets her upon his entering your offices with a "Hello" or some other salutation, and occasionally attempts to engage her in conversation beyond that greeting. She reports to me that he has said things to her such as, "It finally stopped raining"; "Did you have a good weekend?"; and, perhaps most offensively, since it is clearly and unmistakably a comment on her personal appearance, "I like that jacket." Moreover, when Mr. Katz prepares to take his leave of your offices — often after making my client visibly uncomfortable with his advances — he adds insult to injury with a "Good-bye," or occasionally the inappropriately familiar "'Bye now."

Dr. Katz, perhaps you have told yourself that Mr. Katz's comments are innocuous, or that he "means well." It's quite possible that if I were in your position, e.g., a man whose only son is a "problem," I would attempt to convince myself of the same thing. But harassment is in the eyes of the harassee. I'm sure you'll agree that Ms. Silverstein is an extraordinarily sensitive and empathetic young woman — that is no doubt why you hired her, to provide balm to your patients even before their "treatment" sessions begin — and while she puts a brave face on the situation, it is obvious to me that your son's constant hounding is beginning to wear her down. You have probably noticed that, unlike other receptionists, she rarely hums cheery songs to herself or hangs up colorful posters of animals photographed in amusing poses. Now you know why.

My client is not contemplating any action against you or Mr. Katz at this time. I might add that this is her decision, made against my express counsel, prompted no doubt by the enormous goodwill she feels toward you. She seems to believe that a simple but substantial increase in salary would offset the mental and emotional trauma she has suffered, although with more experience in these matters, I know that it is far more likely to require years of expensive employer-subsidized therapy. No matter. You'll no doubt want to try giving her that salary increase to see if it does the trick. It's what a prudent man would do, I suppose, although my personal preference would be for this matter to be resolved in court. In any case, I deemed it incumbent upon myself to bring this matter to your attention, so that you may take immediate steps to correct the grievous injustice being done my client. If your actions fail to alleviate the problem, well, at least we both have this document as evidence that you tried.

Sincerely yours,

Andrew Urquhart, Esq.
Ames, Ames, Urquhart and Fieldsmith
Attorneys-At-Law

cc: National Organization for Women
Take Back the Night
The Lorena Bobbitt Foundation

Ben, I thought it might be fun if we drew up five-year plans. Just as a sort of general guideline. What do you think of this?

JONATHAN'S FIVE-YEAR PLAN

Get office painted

Help Ben find an apartment

Start an exercise program and really stick to it this time

Help Ben find a job

Get out and meet people more

Reevaluate fee structure

Get into birding

Take evening classes — art appreciation? German lit?

Get one of those massaging backrests for the car

Have that mole looked at

How about you, Ben? Let's see your five-year plan! For fun!

Dad, what's the point? This is the sort of thing the Soviet Union used to do. Look what happened to them.

Dr. Katz's Mental Health Club

'Work Out While You Work Things Out!'
'Where the going gets tough and Your psyche gets buff!'
'A New Approach Combining Exercise and Therapy'
'And Don't Forget Our Snack Bar for Healthful Drinks and Munchies'

Relationship Treadmill

It happens again and again. You get into a relationship, reach the threshhold of true intimacy, and then You pull back. Soon it feels like You're walking and walking and just getting nowhere. So why not hop on the RELATIONSHIP TREADMILL and put all that walking to good use? If You're going to squander Your best Years on dead-end romances, You might as well get some aerobic benefit out of it.

Stair Stomper

Frustrated? Resentful? Just plain angry? Climb aboard the STAIR STOMPER and work those feelings out. Just like a regular Stair Stepper, except You stomp on it -- over and over again, all the while picturing the people who make You so mad! Burns far more calories than plain old seething.

Emotional Weight Machine

Your parents. Your siblings. That girl in college who broke your heart. Your first husband. Your children who mock you... these people sit piled atop of your psyche like so many cold, sodden blintzes. The least they can do is provide you with some muscle tone. Each time you add five pounds on our EMOTIONAL WEIGHT MACHINE, visualize it as one more rotten family member/ex-lover/betraying friend whose butt you will soon be able to kick!

Vortex of Self Pity

Okay, so it's a regular old whirlpool bath. But isn't VORTEX OF SELF PITY a cool name? Let the churning waters counteract your roiling emotions, or something.

Dad, I've got a lot more ideas. Don't you think venture capitalists will eat this up??

Find out how Ben learned about venture capitalists!

Dear Julie,

I can't stop thinking about what happened the other day. And I want you to know that I am truly, truly sorry about it. Truly, Julie. Hey, I wouldn't be surprised if there's a song in there somewhere. You probably couldn't care less, could you?

Julie, you must believe that I meant no offense. You and I have always had an easygoing relationship: I stop by the bar after work for a drink, we talk about our day, I tell you a couple of jokes, and then Stanley comes in and ruins the conversation with his banal observations about pothole repair. Whatever. The point is, I <u>always</u> tell you jokes. It's part of the weave of our relationship. Did you know our relationship had a weave? It's a nice tight weave, too, not one of these half-baked machine-made weaves done overseas. When it comes to our friendship, Julie, you can always look for the union label. It says we're able to make it in the U.S.A.

I'm having a little trouble coming to the point. I don't know if you can tell. But here goes: that joke about the bartender and the kangaroo was in no way meant to reflect upon you, or your profession, or your attitude toward marsupials or any other category of animal. As Freud said, sometimes a kangaroo is just a kangaroo. Let's review: a kangaroo walks into a bar and orders a vodka gimlet. The bartender says that'll be six dollars, and as he brings over the drink he remarks that "We don't get many kangaroos in here." The kangaroo replies, "And at these prices, you won't get many more, either." The humor of the joke comes from several sources: a talking kangaroo. Funny. A drinking kangaroo. Funny. A drinking kangaroo whose cocktail of choice is a vodka gimlet. Funny. The word "gimlet." Funny. A bartender who sees nothing odd about a talking, drinking kangaroo. Funny. A bartender who engages said kangaroo with a more or less standard "human" conversational gambit. Funny. And a kangaroo who not only talks, drinks and prefers vodka gimlets, but is also sensitive about the price of a drink: Funny! You see? <u>None</u> of it is meant to dishonor or ridicule the profession of bartending in any way, shape or form. And when I call it a profession I mean every word of it, Julie. To my mind, bartenders are the unsung heroes of urban life. Professional heroes.

Your point about the profusion of bartender jokes in our culture is well taken. Right off the bat I can think of the one about the piano-playing cat and the singing mouse, and the one about the mathematician, the architect and the salesman and their three dogs, and the one about the man picking his teeth and repeating "Boy, can she drive," and the one about the man who claims he can sing out of his — but I'm getting sidetracked. The point is, why are all these jokes set in bars? Not to ridicule bartenders. On the contrary, it's because bars are where jokes are told. Why? Because people feel relaxed and friendly in bars. And who makes them feel that way? Bartenders!!!!

So again, I apologize for unwittingly offending you, but please think of it this way: a joke about a bartender is a <u>celebration</u> of bartenders, a way of saying, "Thank you, favorite bartender, for enriching my life in the way you have."

And remember, Julie, that when I tell a joke it is never my intention to offend — only to amuse. Next time I see you I'll tell you the one about the pope, Yasir Arafat and the blind nurse's aide.

Your friend (I hope!),
Jonathan

All right, Dad, here it is. I still don't get the point, but at least now you can stop bugging me.

BENJAMIN KATZ: THE NEXT FIVE YEARS

Cash in savings bonds

Upgrade stereo

Watch entire "Die Hard" trilogy in one night

Bring back library book

Major-market full-saturation vertical push on Dad's self-analysis video (not sure what this means)

Get up in time for the $2 movie matinee -- save money!

Get one of those mini-satellite dishes

Learn Dad's business for eventual takeover

Have baseball card collection appraised

Interesting vacations

Open retirement account (get seed money first)

Maybe we should have started with a one-week plan and worked up to this.

8

9

0

11

12

1

2

3

4

5

6

STOP HURTING YOUR OWN FEELINGS!

Bringing Who We Are Together with Who We Want to Be
to Watch a Tape of "The Way We Were"

(Note to Self: Got to fix that subtitle!)

By Jonathan Katz, M.D.

3RD DRAFT

CHAPTER ONE: I KNOW WHO I WANT TO BE, AND IT ISN'T YOU

Ours is a society the like of which has never been seen on
this green and blue ball we call earth. We enjoy a level of
physical health unsurpassed in history. We take for granted a
bounty of foodstuffs so great we even have artificial fat --
how many cultures can boast an advancement like that?
Technological breakthroughs in the fields of medicine,
communications and transportation have opened up a staggering
array of choices in virtually every aspect of our lives,
particularly to those of us with satellite dishes.

And yet, in the face of all these miracles, so many of us
feel an emptiness that we cannot explain. A tiny voice inside
us is saying, "Something's missing." And if we could only
diminish the distractions, the "noise" of our day-to-day
living, and listen to that tiny voice, who knows what else it
might tell us? Perhaps that tiny voice would say, "The rewards
you seek are within reach -- but you must know where to look."
Perhaps that tiny voice would say, "Only when you have accepted
yourself can you begin to accept the world around you." Perhaps
that tiny voice would say, "I am Zargon, leader of an
exploratory contingent from star band L-78 in the Freenus
quadrant. We are a minuscule race of time-traveling beings and
our navigational systems have been thrown off by the powerful
signaling devices you Terrans call your beepers. Thus we have
inadvertently landed our tiny ship amid the anterior lobes of
your brain. You must contact the Cluster's molecular surgeons
and remove our craft from your cranium before its synaptic
connections trigger a chain reaction within our power source
and Blooey! No head. It's your only chance -- and you'll have
to travel ten centuries into the future to do it."

Johnny Stunn bit down hard on his cigar butt and thought
about what he had heard. Underneath the patch, there was a dull
ache in the place where his left eye had been. Well, he was
wanted for questioning regarding several unexplained deaths in
this century. He thought about all those bodies, all that
blood. He replayed the scene in his mind until he came to the
wreckage that had once been Terry, sweet, beautiful Terry, and
then he shut the thought off like a faucet.

What did he have to lose? He flipped open his belt-buckle
terminal, jacked in, and he was out on the Matrix.

Something keeps going wrong. How does Chopra do it?

Hello. You have reached the office of Dr. Katz. We are unable to take your call right now because it's after office hours, or my assistant is away from the phone, at lunch, out sick, on a job interview, taking advantage of post-holiday department store sales, Jazzercising, seeing the early-bird matinee, trying to beat traffic out of town for the long Halloween weekend, tanning or suffering a finger spasm. If you're calling from a Touch-Tone phone, please press one now. If not, please wait for the beep and leave a brief message.

If you are calling about an emotional problem, press one now.

If you are calling about a billing problem, press two now.

If you are calling to cancel or reschedule an appointment, press three now.

If you are calling to cancel or reschedule a date, press four now.

If you just got back from an extended visit with relatives and this is an emergency, press five now.

If you'd like to have a dream interpreted, press six now.

If you'd like to have reality interpreted, press seven now.

If you have no message but have simply decided to tie up my phone line in an act of displaced aggression, press eight now.

If you have discovered something important about your sexual orientation, press nine now.

If your spouse has discovered something important about your sexual orientation, press zero now.

If you have assaulted an officer of the law, press star-one now.

If you are calling because someone wants you to make a commitment, press star-two now.

If you are calling because someone wants to have you committed, press star-three now.

If you'd like to hear a brief excerpt from the Katz and Jammers' new CD, "Direct Reimbursement," press star-four now.

If this is a complaint about my assistant, press star-five now.

If this is a complaint about my son, press star-six now.

If this is a complaint from my assistant about my son, press star-seven now.

If you are calling because you just want to pound someone, press the pound sign now.

If you'd like to hear these choices again, please ask yourself what it is you're really trying to avoid. Thank you for calling the office of Dr. Katz!

Dear Ben,

Thank you! for the wonderful little birthday gift. An "electronic diary," eh? Now I'll be able to record my innermost feelings about electronics! No, I'm kidding, I know what it is, of course. You enter in phone numbers and appointments and things like that. In fact I've already been trying it out here and there, and it makes me feel very "cyber." That's the word, right?

Not that I'm claiming to have mastered it! I punched in the phone number for the Chinese restaurant, but when I tried to retrieve it later so I could order some shrimp with snow peas, instead I got a readout of what days of the week July Fourth falls on through the year 2050. I have no idea how that happened. If it had been the Chinese New Year, at least it would have made some kind of sense. Anyway, the good news is that we've got a lot of three-day weekends to look forward to. (By the way, there was another date already entered into the calendar function through perpetuity. It's nice to know what day your birthday falls on in the year 6666, but do I have to start thinking about a present yet?)

Anyway, it's a great gift. Please don't be upset if I don't start using it right away. It's going to take me some time to type the names and numbers from my old organizer into this thing. I appreciated your suggestion that I ask Laura to do it, but I think we both understand the many dangers inherent in that path. For all I know, there may be some way these things can be rigged to explode.

By the way, you can delete phone numbers too, right? Because who needs an organizer to remind you of dates that didn't work out? That's what waking up at three a.m. is for!

That's a joke. Please don't repeat it to your mother.

Anyway, Benjy (may I call you Benjy on this occasion, for nostalgia's sake? I know you made me stop doing that years ago, but it's been quite a while since they put out one of those movies about the dog), receiving a birthday gift from your grown son is a bittersweet event. It reminds me of my greatest, proudest achievement — my wonderful child — but it also leads to the inevitable observation: if I've got a grown son, then I must be getting a bit long in the tooth myself. Mind you, I feel great. I may flatter myself, but I don't think I've ever looked better (oh sure, maybe twenty years ago I had a bit more hair and a little less around the middle, maybe I didn't have a tiny "jowly-wowly" and I hadn't yet developed that hint of a stoop I've been noticing lately, but those are superficial indicators, Ben. I'm talking about inner handsomeness). Even so, there's no denying the passing parade. Occasions like this naturally tend to make one think about the future. There's so much I wish for you, son, so much I want to see happen for you. Much of it would be facilitated by gainful employment on your part, but let's not mar the day by pressing each other's "hot buttons."

Anyway, thanks again, Ben. With this gift I feel like I've "entered the '90s." (It's still the '90s, right?) I think I'll hang on to my old organizer for a while longer — it's a great place to keep important pieces of correspondence, as well as my notes for some of the exciting projects I'm working on — but I can't wait to sit down at a business lunch and pull your gift out the way I've seen the other power brokers do so many times. It may take a while (you know we therapists don't get invited to many business lunches), but that will just prolong the anticipation.

So from your old Dad, thanks for making this birthday special. And I appreciate the sacrifice it must have been for you, considering that you have no real source of income. You must have been saving for quite a long time to be able to afford this on your allowance. Oops, sorry, almost forgot. Your marketing consultant's retainer.

By the way, Ben, if you wouldn't mind, keep your eyes open. I seem to have misplaced my American Express card.

Love you!

Dad

TODAY

TIME ▼

7	15 30 45
8	15 30 45
9	15 30 45
10	15 30 45
11	15 30 45
12	15 30 45
1	15 30 45
2	15 30 45
3	15 30 45
4	15 30 45
5	15 30 45
6	15 30 45

Special thanks to:

Art Bell, Frank Quinn, Kara Welsh, Amy Einhorn, Greer Kessel, Donna Ruvituso, Donna O'Neill, Suzan Kaitz, Bonnie Burns, Tim Braine, Melissa Bardin, Jennifer Rudolph Walsh, Niki Herbert, Loren Bouchard, Roger Gorman and everyone at Reiner Design.

Animators:

James Fagerquist, Annette LeBlanc Cate, Karen LeBlanc, Richardo Luongo, Mark Usher, Kristen Kempton, Martha Williams Akers, Amy MacDonald, and Carol Vidinghoff.

7

8

9

10

11

12

1

2

3

4

5

6

An Original Publication of POCKET BOOKS.

POCKET BOOKS, a division of Simon & Schuster Inc.
1230 Avenue of the Americas, New York, NY 10020

ISBN: 0-671-00318-6

First Pocket Books trade paperback printing October 1996

10 9 8 7 6 5 4 3 2 1

POCKET and colophon are registered trademarks of Simon & Schuster Inc.

Cover Art by James Fagerquist.
Design by Leah Sherman/Reiner Design

Printed in the U.S.A.

For orders other than by individual consumers. Pocket Books grants a discount on the purchase of 10 or more copies of single titles for special markets or premium use. For further details, please write to the Vice-President of Special Markets, 1633 Broadway, New York, NY 10019-6785 8th Floor.